I0123739

Indigenous Media Activism in Argentina

Exploring Indigenous activism through the lens of media practices, this book examines the Indigenous media that has emerged in Argentina since the introduction of legislation in 2009 intended to promote diversity and access in radio and television media production.

Francesca Belotti provides insights into the political and cultural matrix, attitudes of resistance and empowerment, and the outward and inward direction of Indigenous activism by unpacking the media practices that unfold in Indigenous radio and television stations in Argentina. The theoretical framework combines studies on indigeneity, social/decolonial movements and media practices, and draws on interviews conducted with media practitioners from different Indigenous populations around Argentina. The book examines how media practices support and sustain Indigenous political and cultural activism and the process of ethnic identity self-ascription. It also addresses the complex negotiation between indigenising media and assimilating the mainstream, as well as coping with other practical constraints.

This book will be of interest both to students and scholars of Indigenous Studies, Decolonial and Postcolonial Studies, Cultural Studies, Latin American Studies, Media Studies and Social Movements Studies, as well as media activists and practitioners globally.

Francesca Belotti holds a PhD in Political Language and Communication from Sapienza University of Rome. Her research, carried out between Europe and Latin America, focuses on alternative media practices of grassroots organisations, ranging from Indigenous communities to feminist and climate movements. She also investigates everyday digital media usage practices by older and young people, with a focus on ICT-related sexism and ageism. Her work has been published in *New Media & Society*, *Ageing & Society*, *Violence Against Women*, *Media, Culture & Society*, *Latin American Perspectives*, *Ethnicities*, among others.

Media and Communication Activism: The Empowerment Practices of Social Movements

Series editors: Claudia Magallanes Blanco, Alice Mattoni, and Charlotte Ryan

This Routledge series edited by Claudia Magallanes Blanco, Alice Mattoni, and Charlotte Ryan grapples with recurring issues facing practitioners, teachers, students, and scholars of communication activism; it addresses challenges to communication activism as well as emancipatory practices that build culturally resonant, richly networked, multi-faceted, movement communication systems. Core series themes include:

- The power structures of media and communication activism;
- Rights in the framework of media and communication activism;
- Outcomes, learning and sustainable futures in media and communication activism.

This is a global series published in English, and the editors welcome submissions from authors who work primarily in other languages.

Beyond Prime Time Activism
Communication Activism and Social Change
Charlotte Ryan and Karen Jeffreys

Contesting Austerity and Free Trade in the EU
Protest Diffusion in Complex Media and Political Arenas
Julia Rone

Indigenous Media Activism in Argentina
Francesca Belotti

For more information about the series, please visit: www.routledge.com/ Media-and-Communication-Activism/book-series/MCA

Indigenous Media Activism in Argentina

Francesca Belotti

R Routledge
Taylor & Francis Group

NEW YORK AND LONDON

First published 2022
by Routledge
605 Third Avenue, New York, NY 10158

and by Routledge
4 Park Square, Milton Park, Abingdon, Oxon, OX14 4RN

Routledge is an imprint of the Taylor & Francis Group, an informa business

Library of Congress Cataloging-in-Publication Data
A catalog record for this title has been requested

ISBN: 978-1-032-15183-0 (hbk)
ISBN: 978-1-032-15218-9 (pbk)
ISBN: 978-1-003-24308-3 (ebk)

DOI: 10.4324/9781003243083

Typeset in Times New Roman
by Apex CoVantage, LLC

Contents

Acknowledgements

First of all, I would like to thank all the Indigenous media practitioners I met in Argentina, both those who welcomed me and allowed me to get to know their territories and battles, and those who made me work hard for this opportunity, thus forcing me to be vigilant with my research practices. Without all of you, I would not have been able to fully understand the transformative power of the Indigenous life forms and to relate them in this book. Special thanks go to Óscar Moreno, José Sajama and Olga Kuripan for sharing enriching thoughts and moments with me, and to Emilse Siares for teaching me how to tiptoe my way into the Indigenous world, helping me with data collection and processing, and supporting me every step of the way. My gratitude also goes to Alejandro Pérez and all the comrades of the Red Nacional de Medios Alternativos de Argentina who opened my eyes to the significance of alternative broadcasting communication, as well as to the team of the Centro de Producciones Radiofónicas de CEP-PAS Argentina who helped me understand the state of health of Indigenous rights in Argentina. Without you, I would not have been able to reconcile my research work with my activist commitment and constantly reflect on this bridge between two worlds that are often too far apart. For this very reason, I want to thank Claudia Magallanes-Blanco for combining knowledge production and political struggle with determination, self-reflexivity and consistency: you are a role model for me. Thank you for guiding me on this editorial journey and for believing in my work from the beginning. My special thanks also go to Charlotte Ryan and Alice Mattoni, for standing by my side in this process with invaluable insights. All three of you have been my *comadres* just as Charlotte promised me a few years ago when we met for the first time. Thanks also to Martín Becerra and his research team at the Universidad Nacional de Quilmes for supporting me and always respecting the freedom of thought and action required by my job. I would also like to thank my colleague Magdalena Doyle from the Universidad Nacional de Córdoba for the nice exchanges about Indigenous-mediated communication we had, and Freya Schiwy of the University of California for sharing enriching reflections. Also, thanks to Mauro Cerbino and Isabel Ramos of FLACSO-Ecuador for having introduced me, ten years ago, to the strand of studies on community, alternative and popular communication in Latin America. I would like to conclude by thanking Maria Stella Agnoli, Francesca Comunello, Simone Mulargia and Mireia Fernández-Ardèvol, who over the years have taught me how to do research with methodological rigour and analytical depth, never lacking in smiles and friendship.

Introduction

My interest in Indigenous media dates back to 2013. I was in Ecuador and Bolivia studying the political transformations of the early 2000s, the role played by Indigenous and other social movements in them, and the recognition of the *Buen Vivir* rights in the two new Constitutions. I was fascinated by the political agency of those movements and their transformative capacity. What surprised me the most was how immediately these events brought about a radical reform of national media systems. Both the 2011 *General Law of Telecommunications, Information and Communication Technologies* in Bolivia and the 2013 *Organic Law of Communication* in Ecuador recognised the rights of Indigenous communities and social organisations to run 'community media' alongside state-owned public media and private commercial media, with one-third of the radio spectrum reserved for them. At the time, I was familiar with European 'pirate radio,' and had collaborated with some independent online news agencies in Italy, but an Indigenous community running a radio, or a collective having its own TV studio by law, was something completely new for me.

I traced the genealogy of these reforms and discovered that both were inspired by the Argentinian *Law 26,522 on Audio-Visual Communication Services* (LSCA), approved in 2009 under the Kirchner government and fully effective until Macri's rise to power at the end of 2015. This law was pioneering in Latin America in recognising marginalised social sectors (such as Indigenous communities or non-profit social organisations) as providers of audio-visual communication services; this alone made it worth studying to understand the social processes and political conditions that can support a legal change of this magnitude. Even more surprising was that this change appeared in a country like Argentina that was accustomed to portraying itself as a nation '*sin indios*' and yet became the first to legally recognise the Indigenous peoples' right to communication. How had this happened? What political players and interests motivated this reform?

DOI: 10.4324/9781003243083-1

I was also curious to examine why the Argentinian law differed from the Bolivian and Ecuadorian laws, where Indigenous and community broadcasters belonged to the same third media sector, whereas in Argentina the former were treated as public but non-state media (as with Catholic media) and the latter as private but non-profit media (together with a heterogeneous array of associations). Both types of media share social and non-profit purposes, cultural programming and the historical subaltern position of those who run them, i.e., Indigenous communities, social organisations and political collectives (Cerbino & Belotti, 2018), and yet in Argentina they belonged to separate legal categories. Why differentiate between media which were, to my mind, similar?

Furthermore, the mechanisms for both radio frequency allocation and public funding established by the LSCA motivated me to examine how these broadcasters were actually operating. I did not understand why Indigenous communities obtained direct authorisation to broadcast, while social organisations had to participate in a public competition;[1] yet both providers were subject to the same competitive regime to obtain public funding.[2] It seemed contradictory to me to grant public legal status to Indigenous media but then entrap them in the procedures established for the private sector. I also found it ineffective to force Indigenous and community media to undergo complex competition procedures, knowing that these entities thrive on fluidity and spontaneity, and that their communication projects are unlikely to be encased in the templates and language of bureaucracy. What power games and political will were hidden behind these contradictions?

These sparks of interest took me to Argentina in 2016. Funded by the National Scientific and Technical Research Council of Argentina (CONICET) and hosted by the National University of Quilmes (Buenos Aires), I carried out a qualitative research project to explore the experience of Indigenous media under LSCA implementation. Martín Becerra's supervision was essential in contextualising my investigation within the cutting-edge studies on communication policies that his research team has been conducting for years. Moreover, my participation in the National Network of Alternative Media of Argentina (RNMA) was solid preparation in training me to operate media, in understanding the political context and, generally speaking, in approaching the Indigenous world. In particular, Emilse Siares, a member of RNMA, collaborated with me throughout the project and participated in data collection, processing and analysis. At the time, she was working on her original, un-published honour's thesis on two Kolla radio stations operating in the provinces of Salta and Jujuy and helped fill many gaps in my knowledge of the Indigenous world.

Ultimately, I went to Argentina to explore what Indigenous peoples do with media and to understand if and how they differ from community broadcasters (see Belotti, 2020); however, over time I discovered and learnt much more.

Learning About Indigenous Activism Through Their Media Practices

This book synthesises my experience witnessing Indigenous activism in Argentina as conducted through the media. Indigenous media can be broadly defined as the communication processes and projects carried out by, with and/or about Indigenous peoples through/within media platforms, for the purpose of building discourses and practices that support their cultural, political, economic and social claims for self-determination and self-representation (Magallanes-Blanco & Ramos-Rodríguez, 2016). In my research experience, the media has functioned as an electronic portal through which I could glimpse the Indigenous world and observe their "efforts to assert their rights to self-representation, governance, and cultural autonomy after centuries of assimilationist policies, subjugation and marginalisation" (Ginsburg, 2016: 582).

The reflections distilled in this book take an analytical step beyond my original research exploring how and why Indigenous peoples 'do media' (Belotti, 2020). Here, I aim to deepen the understanding of indigeneity, its lifeforms and struggles, by looking at the way media-making supports Indigenous activism in all its expressions. In doing so, this book seeks a space of enunciation which is different for being rooted in the Indigenous territories through which I travelled, in the persons of Indigenous media practitioners I met, as well as in my own experiences navigating the borders between academy and social movements, borders that I sought to blur. The book attempts to provide an additional, distinctive space for asserting the independent claims of Indigenous media. It makes their efforts visible through the lens of my experience as a "humanising endeavour . . . for our participation [as researchers] in the larger political project for social transformation" (Darder, 2018: 96).

Throughout the book I investigate *media practices* as the building blocks for a wide array of emancipatory strategies of Indigenous peoples in Argentina in the *three main fronts* where I saw them at work:

- *Territory*, understood as the natural space in which Indigenous communities live and to which they relate holistically based on their own cosmogonies; to be defended from the extractive and/or polluting interferences of the state and private companies.
- *Culture*, understood as the symbolic space defined by the beliefs, traditions, rituals, knowledge and languages of Indigenous communities; to be rescued from the invisibility to which they have been relegated by Western/Northern cultural homogenisation.
- *Media management*, understood as the operational space in which Indigenous communities apply values and principles that identify their

ethnic affiliation to everyday media-making while dealing with the opportunities and constraints of a media system based on mainstream logic and formats.

In each of these areas, I noticed that Indigenous media activism ran along *three main axes*: a *cultural and political matrix*; an *outward and inward direction*; and a *confrontational and propositional attitude*. The first axis refers to the interplay between political agency and cultural intervention through which Indigenous people " 'talk back' to structures of power that have erased or distorted [their] interests and realities" (Ginsburg, 2011: 240) with politics being the basis of everyday life and culture representing its actual strength (Tuhiwai-Smith, 1999). The second axis derives directly from the position of the media as a 'cultural interface' (Nakata, 2007), that is, osmotic spaces where Indigenous and Western/Northern worldviews meet/clash and hence overlap, intersect and oppose each other at the factual level of cultural discourses and performances. The third axis relates to the very essence of 'decoloniality' (Walsh, 2018), understood as an attempt to challenge the colonial influence on each field it has infiltrated and to counteract it with alternatives informed by Indigenous lifeforms and values.

Media Activism in Latin America and the Importance of Broadcasting

These analyses sit within studies on media activism, understood as the complex and intricate relationship between social movements and communication technologies (Trerè, 2019), with media being 'the lifeblood' of such movements by enabling collective and emancipatory communication practices which challenge the status quo, including established media (Downing, 2018). I refer to theoretical and empirical contributions bridging the study of social movements and media studies (see Mattoni & Trerè, 2014) which investigate the hands-on approach deployed by grassroots groups to challenge the communications system from the ground up, in order to communicate on their own terms, gain power and bring about change in the social and cultural domains (Rodríguez, 2001; Milan, 2016). According to this perspective, media are both "a set of social processes that intersect with protest mobilisations" (Mattoni, 2017: 495) and collective subjects of political contention forming around communication technologies (Gerbaudo & Trerè, 2015; Stephansen, 2017).

In Latin America, this field of study has focused on specific experiences due to the peculiarities of the political history of the region, geo-political dynamics and socio-cultural diversity. I refer to the fertile tradition of research on what Downing (2018) calls 'nanomedia,' that is, the subversive and small-scale analogue media encompassing community, alternative, participatory, citizen and popular broadcasters. Vinelli (2010) speaks about a 'Latin American heritage' in naming these experiences and emphasises the "practical and perceptual mould that deeply marks much current social movement media practices in the region" (p. 28). Latin American grassroots media bind together communication and politics, produce new community-based social relations and alter power relations in the cultural domain (ibid.). They are tools and spaces for political intervention and social change that mark an area of cultural production articulating communication and political struggle through autonomy and organisation (Gumucio-Dagron, 2001; Vinelli, 2014; Cerbino, 2018). These forms of media arise as additional practices of resistance by historically marginalised sectors (Kaplún & García, 1987; Martín-Barbero, 1981; Beltrán & Reyes, 1993; Mata, 2011) which contest hegemonic economic, social and cultural patterns as a citizenship performance enacted through the media (Rodríguez, 2001). They also challenge mainstream media logics (Gumucio-Dagron, 2005; Kejval, 2009) while influencing the state policies that regulate national media systems (Segura & Waisbord, 2016). International analyses reveal the radical positioning of these media, which relies on their territorial and social anchorage (Downing, 2001; Atton, 2002; Carpentier & Scifo, 2010), the participatory processes they activate within the local communities they serve and in which they are embedded (Carpentier, 2007; Scifo, 2015) and the networking capacity they show when interconnecting local struggles at the global level (Howley, 2005). Their alter(n)ative character has been emphasised as anti-systemic positioning and as a struggle for media power (Atton, 2002; Couldry & Curran, 2003; Coyer, Dowmunt, & Fountain, 2007).

This strand of studies has the merit of appreciating the topicality of broadcasting media for communities and movements (including the Indigenous) that struggle against the marginalising effects of global capitalism and neo-liberal policies. I am aware that nowadays media activism focuses mainly on the digital and social media; these have also received more attention from international scholars with substantial theoretical contributions (Castells, 2009; Bennet & Segerberg, 2012; Bakardjieva, 2015, among others). In Latin America too, many scholars have explored how these platforms have been progressively integrated as additional spaces to organise collective protest actions and express identity claims (Trerè & Magallanes-Blanco, 2015; Sierra-Caballero & Gravante, 2017, among others). Exemplary case studies of Indigenous appropriation of digital and social media have ranged from the Zapatista movement in Chiapas (Froehling, 1997; Russell, 2005, among many others) to the Mapuche people in Chile (Salazar, 2002; Hernández, 2020, among others).

However, broadcasting media are still pivotal in individual and collective communication systems and are particularly important for social movements and Indigenous organisations as they are seamlessly embedded in and committed to the territories. Such organisations march to the beat of their own drum, altering the monolithic communication strategies and media content of the mainstream broadcasters, which remain privileged by the general public. They survive within national media systems, like those in Latin America that have historically been a prerogative of corporate lobbies and/or governments, and relegate them to the side-lines (Becerra & Mastrini, 2009; Treré & Magallanes-Blanco, 2015; Segura & Waisbord, 2016).

We should furthermore bear in mind that Internet access and digital literacy are far from universal in Latin America as socio-economic and socio-demographic differences have led to only modest development in the region's digital ecosystem (Galperín, 2017; CAF, 2020). Technological development has taken place alongside the historical processes of social marginalisation (Hernández & Calcagno, 2003) and "raced, classed, and gendered inequalities" (Dutta & Pal, 2020: 2), creating new forms of exclusion for marginalised groups in the form of digital inequalities (Bernal-Camargo & Murillo-Paredes, 2012; Sandoval-Forero, 2013). This means that Indigenous communities in remote geographical areas struggle for connectivity and lack funding to acquire and update media technologies or for training in digital literacy (Wilson, 2015; Ginsburg, 2016). Broadcasting (especially radio) is often all they can afford to break into the mediascape and have a voice.

This is not to take on a 'slacktivist' position since, as a researcher and activist, I have everyday experience of how digital media practices stimulate activism in what is far from piecemeal or low-effort engagement (Dennis, 2018). Nor am I adopting a techno-sceptical stance towards digital media platforms, not least because I reject a techno-deterministic approach that focuses on the consequences of the media for society without considering the connection between the two (in the way of early dystopian and utopian analyses of digital platforms usages, see Wellman, 2004). I am also aware that broadcasting media are connected to digital platforms within a complex media ecology where no one single medium ensures the purity or effectiveness of contentious activities (Treré, 2019). As Ginsburg (2016: 593) argues, "Indigenous media have grown more robust over the last two decades . . . because of the increasing convergence of media forms that blur the boundaries" between platforms and between formats. They "have taken up the pen, the microphone, the camera, and the computer to craft both nonfiction media pieces . . . and fictional narrative media" (Wilson, 2015: 369). They require "a multiplicity of forms of communication, from the performative communication of bodies in the street to the disembodied informational act of texting a meeting time and place communication" to gain "momentum and galvanise collective political action and participation" (Rodríguez, Ferron, & Shamas, 2014: 154).

I have privileged certain media over others simply as the locus of my exploration of Indigenous activism, given also the legal-political framework of my research (I refer to the LSCA, which only regulated the broadcasting media sector; the digital media sector, on the other hand, was governed by the 2014 Law 27.078 known as *Digital Argentina*). Radio stations and TV channels provide "richly contextual human relations that surround media use" (Rodríguez et al., 2014: 152) and allow for a deeper understanding of the reality (with)in which Indigenous peoples (inter)act, including their whole media ecology. Indigenous experiences with these media are particularly fertile in giving an account of media processes, products and relationships, and in placing them within broader social, cultural and political dynamics. Examining grassroots broadcasting media (as is the main focus of studies on community, alternative and popular media) allows us to go beyond punctuated mobilisations (often adopted when it comes to digital activism) and to situate Indigenous media activism within a long-term perspective and anchor it to Indigenous grassroots politics (Mattoni, 2017). It is here that the book adds something to this field of study, in that it illuminates the specific political grievances and grassroots practices of Indigenous peoples, based on their ethnic identity claims, and sustained by broadcasters.

Indigenous Media in Latin America and the Regional Ethnic Resurgence

The media activism lens provides meaningful insights into the militant ramifications of Indigenous media-making in settler-colonial nations. This subject has mainly been addressed through the anthropology of media, a discipline which sees media as cultural products, social processes and arenas of political struggle based on ethnic issues (Spitulnik, 1993). In particular, the idea that the uptake of media should be considered "as an extension of cultural and political activism to establish the presence of Indigenous lives within their own communities, in nation states, and on the world stage" comes from visual anthropology (Ginsburg, 2011: 236). This discipline has historically valued the political implications of Indigenous film-making since the first collaborative ethnographic filming experiences with Indigenous communities (Worth & Adair, 1972; Ginsburg, 1991, 1994; Turner, 1992, 1995) up to the most recent ethnographic works engaged with Indigenous audio-visual productions aimed at supporting the politics of representation of Indigenous culture (Salazar, 2010, 2015).

Cultural and media studies, on the other hand, have paid more attention to the cultural power and political efficacy of Indigenous media production based on radio broadcasting (Wilson & Stewart, 2008), focusing on the way media technologies have been appropriated by small-scale, usually locally rooted Indigenous cultural groups throughout the world (Wilson, Hearne, Córdova, & Thorner, 2014). This book contributes to these strands of study with the specific case of Indigenous radio and video-making in Argentina, a country which is otherwise absent from the genealogy and mapping of Indigenous-mediated communication experiences within Latin America.

Indeed, regional studies on Indigenous media have contextualised the phenomenon within the macro-political transformations in the region since the 20th century. The early experiences of Indigenous-mediated communication date back to the 1950s, when Indigenous spokespersons began participating in radio stations run by peasants and miners as a reaction to the Indigenism of the first half of the century. Both as a paternalistic ideology and modernising state politics, Indigenism treated Indigenous peoples as an exotic minority to be redeemed in order to consolidate nationhood projects based on biological and cultural miscegenation (de la Peña, 1995; de la Cadena, 2008; Svampa, 2016; Tarica, 2016). From the 1960s onwards, an alliance between the Indigenous and proletarian emancipation movements arose as an opposing political ideology, Indianism, which brought together class struggle and ethnic claims (Stavenhagen, 1997). In this transition from one ideology to another, Indigenous peoples found a space on popular radio stations for their own cultural expression and political positions. Doyle (2015a) reconstructs some exemplary experiences, such as *Radio San Gabriel* (Bolivia, 1955), *Radio Onda Azul* (Perú, 1958), *Escuelas Populares Radiofónicas del Ecuador* (Ecuador, 1962) and *Radio Huayacocotla La voz de los campesinos* (México, 1965).

Organised Indigenous resistance consolidated between the 1970s and 1980s, when ethnic identity worked as a unifying link and mobilising agent in many countries (Stavenhagen, 1997). These are the years in which Katarism raised the peasantry's ethnic consciousness and revitalised the Aymara people's political identity in Bolivia (see Rivera-Cusicanqui, 1986 and García-Linera, 2008) and paved the way for the first generation of Aymara intellectuals who formed the Andean Oral History Workshop in 1983 (see Stephenson, 2002). These processes set the foundation for the emergence of the first proper Indigenous media between the mid-1980s and the early 1990s, when Indigenous media practitioners, trained in popular media, realised the importance of managing their own radio and video productions as tools and spaces to serve their own struggles.

In Bolivia, for instance, Sanjinés and the Ukamau Group inaugurated an Andean film production which denounced the labour exploitation, racism and genocide of neo-imperial extractivism, highlighting the cultural foundation of Indigenous resistance (Schiwy, 2018). In Mexico, Indigenous media practitioners appropriated, re-signified and even moved away from top-down programmes aimed at media literacy. These were promoted by the state under the aegis of multiculturalism but were actually informed by a sugar-coated version of Indigenism. In the case of video-making, Wortham (2004, 2013) and Smith (2006) show how Indigenous practitioners emancipated themselves from mainstream standards during the training stage of the Audiovisual Media Transfer Programme for Communities and Organisations. While finding alternative forms to produce and distribute their products, they managed to relocate this state programme's goal from the ground up. Schiwy and Weber (2017) document how Indigenous video transcended the community-based video-making promoted by the state to include 'homegrown, vernacular video-making' and collaborative video art born within resistant communities and political movements. As for radio stations, Cornejo (2002), Ramos-Rodríguez (2016) and Castells-Talens (2011) highlight that the Indigenist projects activated under the System of Indigenous Cultural Radio Stations were appropriated by Indigenous radio practitioners for reactivating and de-archaeologising cultural repertoires while fostering social cohesion within communities. These authors show, however, that this top-down programme also ended up supporting new forms of assimilationism, which limited Indigenous empowerment and exercise of citizenship (Castells-Talens, Ramos Rodríguez, & Chan Concha, 2009). Something similar occurred in Colombia: Murillo's (2008) research experience accounts for the critical use of the radio by local Indigenous organisations as a form of resistance to settler-state nationalism. Cortés (2019) updated analysis on the Misak and Nasa radios, showing how dealing with state recognition has eroded horizontal and intergenerational forms of Indigenous communication. These experiences are situated within a 'multicultural-yet-hierarchical racial order' imposed by the state that, according to Rodríguez and El Gazi (2007), caused Indigenous peoples to adopt a different attitude towards radio, with the Awá, Nasa and Guambiano peoples being the most determined to exploit it as a space for autonomy.

In this same period, Indigenous media practitioners also started to network their experiences and expertise at the regional level. Salazar and Córdova (see Salazar & Córdova, 2008, 2019) analysed the political potential inherent in the alternative transnational circuits of Indigenous video distribution, brought about thanks to the *Coordinadora Latinoamericana de Cine y Comunicación de los Pueblos Indígenas* (CLACPI), which emerged to collect Indigenous audio-visual efforts throughout Latin America with the aim of channelling Indigenous demands for more means of communication. In Bolivia, the first Indigenous-only radio stations began to appear, alongside the emergence of multiple networks of community and

Indigenous radio stations (see Ramos-Martín, 2018). Furthermore, the Indigenous film sector formed around the *Coordinadora Audiovisual Indígena de Bolivia* (CAIB) in 1996. Schiwy (2018) and Zamorano-Villarreal (2017) discuss how this organisation managed to unite media practitioners from different Indigenous peoples across Bolivia to raise funds, organise festivals and disseminate multimedia packages. Schiwy's (2009) analysis stresses the appropriation and re-signification of Western cinematic stylistic elements by Indigenous video-makers, who adjusted their media choices to the Andean cultural politics of decolonisation. Zamorano-Villarreal (2009, 2014), on the other hand, problematises how Indigenous video-making could challenge and, at the same time, contribute to the commodification, exoticisation and spectacularising of indigeneity. Her work converses with Himpele's (2008) analysis of the gradual indigenisation of popular culture in Bolivia. He shows how, although the indigenist project injected romantic images of indigeneity into folklore and popular culture with the paternalistic aim of creating a homogenous middle class, from the mid-1980s onwards Indigenous video-makers in the country were able to appropriate and recycle the forms of popular culture to represent their own cultural identities.

This Indigenous uprising "began out of sight (of the dominant society)" in the mid-1980s but then burst "on to the national and international stages" (Tuhiwai-Smith, 1999: 108) in the early 1990s, when many Indigenous movements refused to participate in celebrations of the fifth centenary of the arrival of European colonisers in America. In this regard, Bengoa (2000) speaks of an 'ethnic resurgence,' with Indigenous peoples demanding the healing of historical ruptures, territorial displacements and the kidnapping of languages and knowledge, and claiming the right to exercise citizenship according to their own ways of life. These were the years of the Zapatista uprising in Chiapas, followed by ethnic-based protests and coalitions in Bolivia and Ecuador, which culminated in the unprecedented constitutional recognition of *Buen Vivir* rights and the election of Evo Morales (the first Indigenous president in the world) in Bolivia and Rafael Correa in Ecuador in the early 2000s. In this same decade, international law began to address ethnic claims under the unifying doctrine of human rights through international agreements, such as the 1948 Universal Declaration of Human Rights, the 1978 UNESCO Declaration and the 2007 Declaration on the Rights of Indigenous Peoples, which acknowledged communication as a human right and declared cultural identity an inalienable right of Indigenous peoples.

These higher political forums allowed Indigenous peoples to force states to reform national regulatory frameworks (Salazar, 2015) while bringing together representatives of various Indigenous peoples to strategise in the face of globalisation (Wilson & Stewart, 2008).[3] Claims against media governmentalisation and concentration were inscribed within these advocacy activities, mainly because the media industry had been giving substantial support to (neo– and post–)colonialism throughout the region (Treré & Magallanes-Blanco, 2015). It was, therefore, also necessary to reform the media sector to recognise Indigenous rights.

This normative and political upheaval provided a major impetus to the proliferation of Indigenous media. Since the mid-1990s, they have multiplied throughout the region, supported also by digital platforms. Along with the pioneering use of the Internet by the Zapatista movement spreading its struggle worldwide (see Castells, 1997; Magallanes-Blanco, 2000; 2011), the *Mapuexpress* website became pivotal for counter-information about the conflict between the Mapuche and the Chilean state (see Salazar, 2003; Gutiérrez-Ríos, 2014). In Bolivia, independent media activists from different ethnic communities created what, since 2009, has been called the *Plurinational Communication System of the Indigenous, First Nation and Intercultural Peoples of Bolivia*, a consensual management body defending Indigenous communication rights (see Salazar & Córdova, 2008; Schiwy, 2018). Since then, several Continental Summits of Indigenous Communication in Latin America have been held over the years, bringing together media practitioners, scholars and activists from different countries to discuss the ways they use media in Indigenous struggles (see Magallanes-Blanco & Treré, 2019).

This genealogy and mapping of Indigenous media in Latin America lacks narratives and analyses about the Argentinian experience, where most Indigenous radio and audio-visual production was consolidated only following the passing of the LSCA. This is not surprising, if we consider that Indigenous peoples in Argentina have been 'erased' from the public eye and discourse under a state policy aimed at denying Indigenous (pre–)existence and autochthony. Indigenous media productions, therefore, were neither relevant nor seen until their legal recognition, making Argentina a unique case study in the region. The most comprehensive analyses about Indigenous media in the country are those of Doyle (2015a, 2015b, 2016, 2018), who reconstructed Indigenous debates on communication rights to contextualise and focus her ethnographic work on the Indigenous sense-making of the right to communication. Her findings concur with Siares' sociological study on Kolla radio stations (Doyle & Siares, 2018), which highlights the link between broadcasters, territory and the need to make Indigenous culture visible. These analyses also resonate with the research findings of Lizondo (2015, 2018), who highlights the collective appropriation and ethnic re-signification of radio management and programming by Indigenous media practitioners. Soler (2017, 2019), on the other hand, analyses the emergence of Indigenous cinema in Chaco as an intercultural space where Indigenous communities respond to the official national history. Finally, Yanniello's (2014) compilation study in Patagonia shows how the Mapuche people make sense of media as a form of resistance that has mutated over time but maintains its ancestral logics and decolonising purpose. All these disaggregated experiences can be better placed within the country-based contextual overview this book provides in reporting about the Indigenous peoples who live, struggle and broadcast in this corner of Latin America. The goal is to make their activism known through the lens of media practices while contributing to theorisations based on praxis.

Outline of the Book

The first chapter of the book treats the key concepts and theoretical approaches I have drawn upon in the analysis of Indigenous media activism (i.e., indigeneity and media decolonisation; media practices and media indigenisation). Following on from this, I provide background information about Indigenous peoples in Argentina, state policies towards them, and the path towards recognition of their communications rights. The overall situation of Indigenous media in Argentina at the time of the inception of the research are then illustrated along with a discussion of both the methodological and epistemological choices adopted when designing and implementing the research project. The chapter concludes with a discussion of the opportunities and difficulties of research committed to social change (as mine sought to be) and the decolonisation path undertaken while working with and for Indigenous peoples.

Chapter 2 analyses the media practices that support the territorial struggles of Indigenous peoples as a fertile battlefield in which decoloniality within and beyond the media can be seen. After tracing the main territorial conflicts involving Indigenous communities in Argentina and thematising them as both an ontological and ontic clash between the colonial and Indigenous conceptions of territory, the chapter gives an account of how Indigenous media practitioners narrate what happens in their lands, how they inhabit them, and finally how they incorporate the territory as a cosmogony into media production. By making territorial struggles known, Indigenous media practitioners give a call to action, thus expanding the scope of protests and linking Indigenous communities struggling in different parts of the country. By participating in these conflicts, they testify to their side of the story of coloniality, thus locating it in the experiences of those who live in and fight for the territory. While doing so, they also embed the territory itself in the media as an additional space and tool for performing the communication and relatedness that spring from the holistic community–Mother Earth relationship.

Chapter 3 explores Indigenous media activism in the field of culture, highlighting from the outset the centrality of communication as a mechanism for reproducing Indigenous cosmogonies and defining other forms of livelihoods and relatedness. The chapter investigates those Indigenous media practices aimed at both promoting these cosmogonies and lifeforms and contesting those of the dominant culture. The first section addresses the centrality of orality in both the intergenerational transmission of knowledge and the collective hi-storytelling within communities, thus highlighting the fundamental role that radio broadcasting plays both for the Indigenous peoples themselves and for colonial society. The second section focuses on the decolonial practice of centring media content production in the everyday life of Indigenous communities as a counter-hegemonic gesture that redefines social priorities and relations while counteracting stereotypes of the Indigenous world. Finally, the last section analyses the multiple meanings of rescuing native languages in Indigenous media programming and concludes with a reflection on the intercultural dialogue that the hybridisation of genres and languages might open up.

Chapter 4 addresses Indigenous activism in the institutional, social and economic sustainability of media as a field of tensions/negotiations with colonial modernity. Firstly, it analyses the internal dynamics of media organisation and management, thus accounting for the extent to which Indigenous media practitioners manage to indigenise inner processes and where Western/Northern standards instead prevail. Secondly, the chapter focuses on the relational dynamics both between young and elderly people and between women and men, thus problematising the interplay between social roles in Indigenous culture and stereotypes related to usages of modern communication technologies. Finally, the chapter explores the coping strategies adopted by Indigenous media-makers to survive in the media system, thus demonstrating their efforts to reconcile militancy with subsistence, and to satisfy the demands of bureaucracy whilst staying true to their political and cultural projects.

The conclusion summarises the lessons from media practices adopted by Indigenous communities in Argentina that may apply to Indigenous and marginalised peoples elsewhere seeking to protect lands, rights, cultures, languages, identities and ways of life. Lest these efforts appear of little import, the reader need only be reminded that such struggles are proliferating across the world as a bulwark of resistance to, and awareness of, the harmful effects of capitalism on relations between people and between humans and nature. Contemporary movements often borrow and co-opt Indigenous ideas to substantiate their claims; therefore, it is worth understanding Indigenous demands more profoundly. Moreover, based on the limitations of the research experience, the conclusion outlines what committed research can do to support Indigenous media in their political activities, thereby enhancing the civic role researchers might play, decolonising the habits of academy and dismantling the ivory tower in which we, as scholars, seclude ourselves.

Notes

1. The allocation of both radio frequencies and public funds was overseen by the former Federal Authority for Audio-Visual Communication Services (AFSCA), created by the LSCA, whose powers were later transferred to the National Communications Entity (ENACOM), created by President Macri's legal amendments in 2016.
2. Indigenous and non-profit media were eligible to participate in the Competitive Development Fund for Audio-Visual Media (FOMECA), consisting of 10% of the taxes paid by commercial licensees.
3. It is worth mentioning that the international agreements ended up regimenting collective human rights according to a legal and political paradigm that eschews strong forms of Indigenous self-determination and privileges and individual civil and political rights (Engle, 2011). Moreover, the problematisation of the negative effects of globalisation on Indigenous lands and cultures has not resulted in a change of trend. Finally, "the incorporation of difference was dictated by the organising logic of whiteness," which formulates diversity "within the logic of neoliberal culturalism" (Dutta & Pal, 2020: 8) rather than disputing the colonial differences.

1 Approaching Indigenous Media in Argentina

Although different in cultural influences and political trajectories, Indigenous communities in Argentina share the need to decolonise both imaginaries about Indigenous peoples and their own inner practices, while defending ancestral territories against local or national government and private companies and recovering their cultural identities against global homogenisation. Media activities are pivotal to support these struggles. For these reasons, this chapter opens with a composite theoretical framework that interweaves studies on indigeneity, decoloniality and media practices, thus placing Indigenous media activism at the forefront of multiple research strands that also bring Latin American literature into dialogue with the European and US ones. After establishing this framework, the chapter traces the Indigenous peoples' trajectory in Argentina and their struggle to take the floor in the media arena. The specificities of the Argentinian case study provide essential background that contextualises and justifies the research design and stance illustrated toward the end of this chapter.

Theoretical Framework

Indigeneity and Media Decolonisation

When approaching Indigenous media, I consider indigeneity from both a constructivist perspective, which focuses on how individuals construct or make sense of social life, and a critical inquiry perspective, which is rooted in a Marxist/socialist theoretical tradition that seeks to challenge oppressive structures (Crotty, 1998). The former sees indigeneity as a social construction based on belonging and differentiation dynamics, with (self–) ascription playing a pivotal role in developing the ethnic identity of a group. In this, I follow the branch of studies that, from Barth onwards, has detached indigeneity from those essentialist conceptions that consider it in racial terms, as a set of static cultural traits, as a mere exercise of aboriginal languages,

DOI: 10.4324/9781003243083-2

or as the absence of modern social attributes (Trinchero, 2009). I prefer to look at indigeneity dynamically, as a relational (self–)identification process in which individual agency intertwines with economic, political and cultural conditions, shaping Indigenous identities within social relationships that involve multiple arenas and actors (Wortham, 2013). The critical inquiry perspective, on the other hand, provides me with the lens of disparities arising from hegemonic and marginalising forces across the world, thus enhancing the oppositional processes that define indigeneity.

By combining constructivism and critical inquiry perspectives, I can situate Indigenous media within their social context, highlighting the proactive processes that build them, especially at the community level (constructivist approach), while also flagging the wider phenomenon of colonial oppression (critical theory approach). These perspectives open up a space to nurture what Albán (2013) calls 're-existence,' that is, the devices that communities create and develop to dignify and re-invent life within the reality established since colonialism. As Ginsburg (1994) explains, indigeneity marks a colonial field of power relations where Indigenous peoples dispute the dominant representation of their own history, land and culture. Colonisation has been depriving Indigenous peoples not only economically but also culturally by repressing their own forms of knowledge production while forcing them to adhere to the hegemonic culture (Quijano, 2000). For this reason, Wilson and Stewart (2008) define a cultural group as Indigenous by highlighting the group's differentiation-based relationship with the colonial power: Indigenous peoples have occupied territories prior to the arrival of occupants, have been perpetuating, negotiating and adapting distinctive cultures and identities and have experienced different forms of subjugation and resistance.

Specifically, in Latin America, indigeneity has been shaped by multiple processes and dynamics over time. As Lizondo (2018) and Soler (2017) synthesise, after European colonisation, the dispossession of Indigenous peoples' lands, cultures and languages has continued under the construction of homogenous republics, which in some cases, such as in Argentina, have even implied the extermination of Indigenous peoples. This is the reason why decolonial scholars – e.g., Escobar, Mignolo, Quijano and Maldonado-Torres, among others – argue that in Latin America colonialism is not a stage but a continuum (i.e., *colonialidad*) that started with the conquest of America and continued with the expansion of modernity. According to these authors, coloniality refers to the reproduction of inequalities and hierarchies based on race, gender and geopolitics, which shape and organise labour, subjectivity, policies and knowledge according to the logic of domination over the other. In this process, nation-states have alternatively stigmatised and marginalised colonised groups as negative and exotic others, or they have assimilated them into mainstream culture by erasing cultural differences (Wilson & Stewart, 2008). Mainstream media have supported them through stereotypical narratives that have either criminalised Indigenous peoples for breaking norms and opposing institutionalised power, or promoted the image of the *indio permitido* who is allowed to be integrated into modern society for fulfilling romantic expectations based on the archaeological past and folkloric expression (Castells-Talens, 2016). In this regard, Rivera-Cusicanqui (2018) speaks about long-standing negotiations between 'the spheres of power' and 'the spheres of community resistance.' She explains that the communities' drive for autonomy "is permanently under the threat . . . of a sort of identity kidnapping . . . by the state" which, aware of "the strategic importance of the *condición india*," boasts of power sharing but ends up sharing crumbs (ivi: 125). This analysis accounts for the contradictions inherent in the political ideologies of the last century in Latin America which, in the shift from Indigenism to Indianism, shaped inadequate public policies and discourses before giving way to the often merely rhetorical doctrine of human rights. The contemporary claims for a right to difference, as Mignolo (2001) argues, was ultimately imposed by the coloniality of power and is now assumed by Indigenous peoples to gain "those rights that have been taken away from them by five centuries of 'external' and 'internal-external' colonialism" (p. 191). The negotiations mentioned by Rivera-Cusicanqui encapsulate these tensions and colonial power relations at work between the Indigenous and non-Indigenous world, highlighting how the former resists the physical and cultural domination of the latter while forging and maintaining a sense of belonging to Indigenous worldviews and practices.

This framework locates my work at the juncture between social/ decolonial movements and media studies, with particular attention to the role of media practices in building counter-hegemonic movements for the self-determination of Indigenous peoples. These movements proliferate in what is known as the Global South, that is, the transnational political subject (made up of spaces, peoples and imaginaries) resulting from the shared experience of subjugation under contemporary global capitalism (López, 2007; Mignolo, 2011; Garland-Mahler, 2017), from which several scholars derive specific practices of both knowledge-building and struggle (Connell, 2007; Cassano, 2012; Santos & Meneses, 2019). Experiencing colonial and post-colonial regimes is a unique mode of encountering the West and the North, which winds along the 'abyssal line' (Santos, 2018), that is, the frontier where capitalism, colonialism and patriarchy, on the one hand, and the struggle and sociability of colonised peoples, on the other, meet or clash. This encounter/clash shapes the context within which emerging social movements develop their politics of social change and resistance (Thompson & Tapscott, 2010; Dutta & Pal, 2020).

In this regard, Walsh (2018: 17) speaks of decoloniality as a practice "*against* the colonial matrix of power . . . and *for* the possibilities of an otherwise." In approaching decoloniality as praxis, she thus highlights the combination of the protest and the prospect of political and cultural practices aimed at dismantling coloniality and promoting alternatives from the ground up. Decolonisation implies affirming the uniqueness of identities while valuing differences over dominant homogenisation; it consists of adopting localised forms of life and knowledge against universalism, thus placing marginalised populations at the centre. Tuhiwai-Smith (1999), on the other hand, conceives of decolonisation as a process that informs the 'politics of self-determination' of Indigenous peoples, along with healing and transformation (understood as crucial strategies of restoration and change) and mobilisation (understood as the political dynamics of resistance and alliance building). Self-determination might be achieved in consequential phases, based on practices of survival ("of peoples as physical beings, of languages, of social and spiritual practices, of social relations and the arts"), recovery ("of territories, of Indigenous rights, and histories") and development (p. 116). For Indigenous peoples in Latin America, all this translates into the concrete need to survive the many aggressions towards their own bodies, territories and lifeforms, as well as the need to network, organise and strategise as political subjects increasing their capacity to set an Indigenous agenda in the public debate (Servindi, 2008).

Indigenous mediated communication has a major role in facing these challenges. As Magallanes-Blanco (forthcoming) argues,

> discursive, visual and sound representations are important to combat the mechanisms of silencing and making invisible of the colonial powers, . . . show how discourses have been used to infantilise or victimise Indigenous peoples in order to diminish their voice and limit the scope of their struggles.

Indigenous media end up being "places of enunciation" which are "ethically and politically positioned against the colonial difference of power from which they arise" (Cerbino, 2018: 145). As Salazar (2009: 508) states, "Indigenous media can be thought of as a defiant form of political activism and more broadly as specific instances of cross-cultural communication" in that they challenge the homogenised and stereotypical narratives about Indigenous peoples provided by hegemonic media and the state. By owning and managing their own media, Indigenous peoples take control of their 'public image' (Córdova, 2011) by making their struggles and daily reality visible. Ginsburg (1991) makes this point clear in stating that Indigenous media assert a cultural positioning, aimed at mediating historical and territorial ruptures, as well as the violation of ancestral knowledge. In that, Indigenous media are pivotal to hosting and revealing both the cultural creativity and political agency of Indigenous peoples (Himpele, 2008). They are both a political tool to build autonomy and physical resistance and a cultural tool to construct identity, counter-narratives and self-representation (González-Tanco, 2016). They enable the discursive and performative exercise of what de la Peña (1995) calls 'ethnic citizenship,' that is, the capacity to be legal interlocutors and, in this way, to reconfigure the public sphere while participating in it. If we apply this definition to the mediated public space, we can see that media allow Indigenous peoples to exercise what Mata (2006) defines as 'communicative citizenship,' that is, the capacity to be subjects of law in the field of public communication. This means that, through their own media, Indigenous peoples gain access to the mediated public sphere as Mapuche, Aymara, Zapotec, and not as Chileans, Bolivians and Mexicans (Salazar, 2010). This allows them to open up and feed what Marcus (2006) defines as an 'activist imaginary,' i.e., "raising fresh issues about citizenship and the shape of public spheres," (p. 6) and in so doing, decolonise them.

When powerful nations impose their cultural practices and legal systems on regions and peoples, they deny those peoples the right to operate as social beings, i.e., to intervene in and change the social order. To challenge such a hegemonic system, Indigenous people must work to create a counter-system that captures their ways of being, ways of inhabiting the world, relating with and understanding it. Therefore, communication practices that support, protect and nurture this identity-building process must be established, within which Indigenous people constantly push back against the hegemonic assumptions and representations of who they are, while proactively strengthening the inner-shared vision of what being Indigenous actually means. As Ginsburg (2016: 582) clarifies, "while cultural, linguistic and historical circumstances certainly differ, similar circumstances wrought by colonial histories are faced by Indigenous communities everywhere and these frequently motivate their uptake of media." Indigenous media, then, operate as a 'cultural interface' (Nakata, 2007), that is, a material and symbolic site where Indigenous activism plays out. Indigenous media practitioners negotiate constraints and possibilities and draw upon their own understanding of what is emerging all around them. This makes media a (real and symbolic) contested domain where Indigenous peoples meet and interact with the non-Indigenous world, thereby negotiating resources and meanings. Media-as-interface are, therefore, a privileged entry point to the Indigenous world.

Media Practices and the Media Indigenisation

In approaching Indigenous media, I have resorted to the constructivist perspective that, from Luckmann and Berger onwards, has conceived communication as an embodied action through which individuals shape a social reality that, in turn, guides, delimits and enables actions themselves (Knoblauch, 2019). Yet, I have also approached media as shaped by social and cultural factors by stressing media choices and negotiations of meanings (Williams & Edge, 1996). In doing so, I have followed the prolific branch of studies that, from Couldry onwards, has applied practice theory to media and communication. I hold together the defining components of media practices that praxeological approaches have relayed: from performance, treated by Schatzki (1997) as an open-ended set of actions enacted by practitioners, to the entanglement between human and non-human performativity (Nicolini, 2012). In particular, Shove and colleagues (2012) emphasise the link between materials, competence and meaning to highlight the heuristic capacity of media practices. According to them, it is rooted in the interweaving between "objects, infrastructures, tools, hardware and the body itself," "understanding and knowledge," and "mental activities, emotions and motivations" (ibid.: 23). Grasping Indigenous media practices, therefore, means considering "the performative linkage between meanings, objects, and activities" (Trerè, 2019: 17) which provides a multifaceted understanding of what Indigenous activists do with media in their specific contexts and situations, and with what implications. Media practices are indeed interlocked with social, economic and cultural conditions (Williams & Edge, 1996) in a mutual shaping relationship that values what people do concretely with media. This approach is also consistent with the longstanding Latin American tradition of studies on mediations, rooted in the work of Martín-Barbero (2006). Shifting from media to mediations, he moved the focus to the cultural negotiations, social interactions and appropriation dynamics that shape the sense-making of media usages, while valuing the political meaning of everyday practices as grassroots resistance to domination, with and beyond the media.

Mattoni (2020) recently described two different approaches to applying practice theory to media activism: the 'media-as-practices' approach, exploring how grassroots media come into being through practices and how activists experience them; and the 'media-in-practices' approach, considering how media practices, among others, nurture different grassroot political practices. While in previous research I have adopted the former approach, following the literature on communication for social change and the tradition of studies on community, alternative, popular and citizen media (Belotti, 2020), here I try to integrate the latter approach to convey a deeper understanding of Indigenous activism and its practices, within and beyond the media. In this, I follow Bakardjieva's (2020) proposal to consider media practices as a 'sensitising concept' through which to view empirical instances by suggesting where (rather than prescribing what) to observe.

This stance is especially needed when approaching the Indigenous world, since communication is constitutively "present in their conceptions about territory, organisational processes, resistances, and plans for life" (Arcila-Calderón et al., 2018: 193). Media practices offer a perfect lens for navigating these territories, processes, struggles and plans without resorting to analytical categories alien to the Indigenous world itself.

Indigenous media produce knowledge from and about the Indigenous world within an organic link with Indigenous social and cultural practices (Schiwy, 2016). This allows Indigenous identity to be reinforced inwardly while defending it outwardly (Wortham, 2004; 2013). Indigenous mediated communication can indeed be considered 'ethnogenetic' (de la Peña, 1995) in that it creates feelings of belonging and social organisation that define new group boundaries and favour cultural hybridisation and resistance. Media facilitate an outwards/inwards exchange from Indigenous practices: outwardly, they allow for the denunciation of Indigenous conditions and advocacy of their own worldviews while creating solidarity networks; inwardly, they enable the reflection, knowledge production and strengthening of Indigenous cultural identity (González-Tanco, 2016). Whichever way we look at it, media operate as "discursive artefacts that construct a reality as much as they mediate it" (Salazar, 2003: 24). They are spaces of information and representation of the Indigenous reality, which, nevertheless, might concretely transform it through the production and circulation of Indigenous discourses and images. Such a performative character of media also has the retroactive effect of encouraging processes of ethnic identity self-ascription, thus sustaining the struggle for self-determination inside and outside communities (Salazar, 2014). In this regard, Magallanes-Blanco (forthcoming) speaks of a 'spiral' of Indigenous communication that wraps around five interconnected dimensions. First, communication reproduces Indigenous cosmogonies, that is, the "systems of thought that expose forms of relationship between subjects and between subjects and the environment, both based on the valorisation of what is human and of nature, over market and progress" (ibid.). Second, this gives rise to self-reflexivity: communication becomes a mechanism for rethinking identity and relations within the communities and with the outside world. Third, it can substantiate a political strategy for deconstructing stigmas, and fourth, it ends up unfolding in the autonomous exercise of a right. Finally, all this precipitates in the media when Indigenous modes of communication (such as assemblies, *mingas*, rituals, legends, dances, storytelling) materialise in technological means (such as stories, plays, songs, radio shows, videos, web pages) "to be circulated within the communities or to bring the voice out" (ibid.).

Even if communication technologies are alien to the Indigenous world and in some cases are handed over by top-down government programmes,

Indigenous peoples can appropriate them according to their need to reflect their cultural practices and to contribute to the movement for autonomy (Wortham, 2004). The appropriation of external technologies as means of communication allows Indigenous peoples to search for their own pluralistic and participatory development, as a right to choose between ancestral and modern communication practices (Otero, 2008). This is where the intertwining of objects, knowledge and sense-making that define media as practices comes to the fore. Indigenous peoples re-signify technologies to reflect their own cultures and construct their own unofficial narrative. This is what Salazar (2002) and Schiwy (2009) call 'media indigenisation' or 'indianisation.' By negotiating between Western conventions/logics and traditional forms of Indigenous communication (Salazar, 2014; Doyle, 2015b), Indigenous media practitioners adapt technologies to their purposes and needs. They incorporate values, protocols and methodologies in media processes and products – what Ginsburg (1991, 1994) calls 'embedded aesthetics.' In doing so, media-makers sometimes incur the risk of 'selling out' or assimilating formats and content (Wilson & Stewart, 2008).

This negotiation detaches Indigenous communication from benevolent, purist and linear conceptions, without undermining the indigenisation process, which is not about changing aesthetics and formats, but rather about breaking the traditional structures of the media system (Schiwy, 2002, 2009). In this regard, Aguirre (2002) speaks about 'ethno-communication,' that is, "the set of experiences of social exchange that allow the circulation of messages marked by the belonging to a cultural base of ethnic origin and mediated by resources eminently pertaining to that same cultural base" (p. 48). Based on intra– and inter-group relations and on symbolic exchanges, Indigenous communication can "give centrality to the basically human character of the communication process" in the media by providing new meanings to the use of the word, incorporating new recipients of the messages (not necessarily men or women but also animals and plants, for example) and even breaking the linearity of the present time (ivi: p. 49). In this way, Indigenous media end up being a form of cultural invention that combines elements of dominant and dominated societies in the use of communication technologies: they are creative tools at the service of new practices of signification (Ginsburg, 1991). Indigenous media practitioners force "the [mainstream] logics of information production and agenda setting, modes of entertainment, media spaces and speaking times," introducing "possibilities of expression from their own languages, from the dynamics of [communities'] everyday life and mode of organisation" (Doyle, 2015a: 105). They do so by incorporating symbols and codes of communality into Indigenous media processes and products, making the intimacy of families newsworthy, and translating the autonomy of Indigenous peoples in images and sounds.

A concrete example of this traditional knowledge embodied in modern technology is reported by Wortham (2013). When *Tv Tamix* broadcasted in Oaxaca (Mexico), the producers thanked the sacred mountain, showed women working in the fields or preparing religious offerings and played the Mixe hymn with images of their recording and editing activities in the studio. In other words, they exhibited their cultural particularities to Indigenous and foreign audiences and visually linked the culture and autonomy of the Mixe people to the use of technological equipment. Something similar can be said about the adoption of the 'integral (or Andean) sequence shot' that Sanjinés adopted in some of his films: he incorporated the collective as the protagonist while introducing in the same shot the present, past and future in accordance with the Andean circular conception of time. The Ukamau Group used this *plano secuencia* to provide the space and time for the collective social agent in front of the camera to enact political memories and social interventions, while the scripted dialogue gave way to improvisation (Schiwy, 2018). Even in the experience of the *Tejido de Comunicación para la verdad y la vida* of the Nasa people in Colombia, analysed by Almendra (2010), cultural and media practices permeate one another. Communication is practised as a textile: its threads are both the traditional mechanisms of community articulation (e.g., assemblies, *mingas*, congresses and mobilisations) and communication technologies (i.e., radio, print, video) that strengthen information inside and outside the community; its nodes are the community members (e.g., teachers, guards, communicators, authorities) and external counterparts (other organisations and allied people) that participate in the emancipatory project; and its holes are the spaces and activities aimed at deliberating about direct actions to implement such a project. This conceptualisation values the interconnection between modes of communication and media, between the inside and the outside of communities, thereby focusing on the web of relationships that inhabit the territory where Indigenous life and struggle are woven.

Such an osmotic process between making cultural objects and forging cultural processes through media practices, this making of communication that involves social practices and vice versa, becomes an effective strategy for the generation of counter-discourses and alternative public spheres. This is what Salazar and Córdova (2008) call the 'poetics' of Indigenous media, which insists on the importance of the process over the product, insofar as it stimulates reflection, debate and analysis of the needs and views of Indigenous peoples. This is what puts the praxeological approach to media back at the centre. Indigenous media are embedded in the forms of life and struggle of Indigenous peoples, while Indigenous cosmogonies inform the way to handle technologies. No wonder that "practitioners have played a central role in the conceptualisation of Indigenous communication processes in the region" by systematising and interpreting their own media practices (Arcila-Calderón, Barranquero, & González-Tanco, 2018: 182). It is ongoing, theorising work that people, communities and movements have carried out "as a recognition of the embodied nature of lived struggles [. . .], outside the colonising gaze" (Dutta & Pal, 2020: 2). *Communication with identity* (CCAIA, 2012) is an example of the Indigenous theorisations that have been reflexively and collectively elaborated by Indigenous organisations in Argentina during the public discussion of the LSCA.

The Argentinian Case Study

Indigenous Re-existence

When approaching Indigenous media in Argentina, the first issue that comes to light is the specific operation of 'otherness formations' (Briones, 2005) that have taken place in this part of Latin America. Briones (2003: 67–70) explains that throughout the region the subordination of Indigenous peoples was intended to "domesticate otherness" through different "practices and policies of decharacterisation of the *other indian*," in which the *mestizaje* was postulated "as [the] epitome and metonymy of the 'national type.'" Instead, the Argentinian model of nationhood never "turned hybridisation into the symbolic capital of the 'national being'" (ibid.). Argentina was historically represented as a 'nation without *indios*,' thus ignoring Indigenous peoples as constitutive of its identity (Trinchero, 2009; Delrio, 2010) and promoting the de-indianisation of the country and its memory (Briones & Delrio, 2007). This annihilation of Indigenous peoples resulted in minimising the deplorable events that occurred under the Spanish conquest in the 16th century, the construction of the nation-state in the 19th century, and the invasion of private capital in the 20th century. I refer to military subjugation, ethnocide, expulsion and subsumption of survivors into the labour force, along with the acculturation programmes that deconstructed the socio-political and economic organisation of Indigenous peoples while endorsing the depredation of their territories and natural resources on which their sustenance relies. While Spanish colonisation primarily occurred in the north-west of the country and in the current provinces of Corrientes and Misiones, justified by the 'civilisation vs. barbarism' imaginary (Gordillo & Hirsch, 2003), the building of the modern nation-state decimated and expelled the Indigenous populations in the Pampa, Patagonia and Chaco regions, known as 'interior frontiers,' that were intended for incorporation into the national territory in order to satisfy the demands of capitalist markets, both domestic and foreign, for resources and labour. If European colonisation had not been brutal enough, a continuum of state violence against Indigenous people can be traced in Argentina from its constitution until today, always legitimised by the assumption that Indigenous peoples were an internal enemy to be eliminated and/or under the aegis of economic interests to be pursued at the expense of those of Indigenous communities.

The first stages of organised social response by Indigenous peoples inhabiting Argentina date back to the 1950s, during an advanced phase of Peronism. According to Lenton (2015), while in the 1940s this had established a 'paternal relationship' with some Indigenous communities in the North-West and Patagonia, and defended their interests against oligarchies or landowners under the aegis of the promotion of labour, after the coup d'état the management of Indigenous issues was delegated to the provinces and thus local governments stopped the restitution of land and even turned a blind eye to illegal appropriations from and labour exploitation of Indigenous peoples. In the 1960s, the military character of the state's indigenist politics was exacerbated while a state discourse based on acculturation and integration gained momentum. It was then, and even more so in the 1970s, that the early Indigenous organisations in Argentina grouped into national and international networks claiming their lands as reparations for the historical debt owed by the state (ibid.). They combined with new Indigenous urban-based movements and peasant or workers' movements from other neighbouring countries, such as Katarism in Bolivia (see Rivera-Cusicanqui, 1986; García-Linera, 2008) and Mapuche organisations in Chile (see Carter, 2010), culminating in transnational meetings with high participation of Indigenous delegates.

In reconstructing the key moments of the Indigenous organised resistance in Argentina, Lenton (2015) reports an initial interference/influence of religious and political sectors but also recognises the Indigenous political agency in the confrontation with both the state and landowners. While emphasising cultural claims, Indigenous organisations were able to define political and legal demands (e.g., land restitution, participation in state bodies, political recognition, transnational networking), which paved the way for post-dictatorship Indigenous grassroots politics (ibid.).

Indeed, with the establishment of democracy, especially since the 1994 Argentinian constitutional reform, Indigenous organisations have mobilised for self-determination and self-management throughout the country, to be recognised as collective subjects of law and to limit state interference in their own decision-making. The pressure from international debates, mainly fostered by the transnational networks of Indigenous organisations, paved the way for significant legal advances, which, however, showed a mixture of multiculturalism and neoliberal entrepreneurship (Cruz, 2017). International agreements, anchoring the dispute for self-determination in communicative sovereignty, forced the Argentinian state to act accordingly. Running an Indigenous medium free from interference and obtaining public funds to sustain media activities represented a real way of breaking out from the state-controlled regime of invisibility historically perpetrated against the Indigenous peoples.

The Struggle to Take the Floor

The Argentinian media system has historically been dominated by four private companies; these have branched out into all the productive chains in almost all the communication industries and have been favoured by public policies adopted by different governments over the decades. They have been the recipients of the state financial support given to the main players to the detriment of other smaller companies (Becerra & Mastrini, 2009). The private, for-profit sector consolidated such an oligopoly in the 1980s and 1990s when non-profit media were made illegal (Kejval, 2009). A few multimedia conglomerates took over the communication industry and turned it into a real business, with the Clarín Group operating as the dominant business group, always endorsed and feared by governments of different political orientations (Mastrini, Becerra & Bizberge, 2021). This is the backdrop against which public discussion and the subsequent passing into law of the LSCA took place in 2009, fostered by the 21-point Coalition for Democratic Broadcasting that since 2004 has brought together different media sectors to build a new and fairer legal framework for regulating the national media system (see Busso & Jaimes, 2011; Segura & Waisbord, 2016).

According to Doyle (2015b, 2016), Indigenous peoples participated in some initial meetings of the 21-point Coalition where they demanded a specific mention of Indigenous media and rights. As this specific debate did not find enough space on the Coalition's agenda, some members of the Mapuche Confederation of Neuquén, with the legal advice of the Human Rights Observatory of Indigenous Peoples and the contribution of other Indigenous organisations,[1] decided to present their own separate proposal. They sought to include Indigenous peoples in the new law as a fourth category of media providers: the non-state public law media, alongside state, commercial and non-profit providers. Hence, the Coordinator of Indigenous Audio-visual Communication of Argentina (CCAIA, 2012) presented a document introducing the notion of 'Communication with identity' aimed at supporting the idea that Indigenous media are an autonomous category that could not be transferred to the state or private sector. This choice was part of a 'differentiation strategy' (Lizondo, 2018) motivated by legal and political-cultural reasons. On the one hand, the Constitution recognises the ethnic and cultural pre-existence of Indigenous peoples, thus ensuring their equality before public entities. The reference to subjects of public law with the 'non-state owned' clarification aimed to distinguish Indigenous communities from the state and limit its power to intervene in the internal life of Indigenous broadcasters and their organisational processes. On the other hand, refusing to merge with the non-profit private media category (which included non-profit and grassroots media) implied the legal recognition of the different political-organisational systems of the Indigenous peoples, relying on a community-based holistic lifeform that is more than associative (as social organisations owning and managing community media are).

Although supported by these arguments, Indigenous representatives had to negotiate with the state during the participatory legislative process and ended up agreeing to incorporate Indigenous media into the public sector, albeit whilst maintaining the "non-state owned" specification. In this way, they had access to the one-third of the spectrum reserved for public media (the LSCA divided it equally between the public, commercial and non-profit sectors) through direct authorisation (instead of by competition, as was the case with non-profit media). Moreover, they could also benefit from diverse and direct funding sources, such as the resources provided by the National Institute for Indigenous Affairs (INAI) and not only from the public Fund for Competitive Development of the Audio-Visual Media (FOMECA), as was the case with non-profit media.[2]

However, a change of government in December 2015 jeopardised the regulation scaffolding, the financing model, and the relations between government and media companies defined by the LSCA. The entire media system was reformed by decree and under the aegis of a rudimentary media convergence paradigm that aimed at restoring a market-based policy (Becerra, 2015). Besides replacing the independent audio-visual and telecommunications regulatory authorities established by the LSCA (known as AFSCA and AFTIC, respectively) with a new agency completely dependent on the Executive (the ENACOM), the decrees directly benefited the largest audio-visual groups and telephone conglomerates. These legal and administrative changes paralysed the granting of the last awarded FOMECA funds, while the political scenario undermined the activities of all broadcasters working on a non-commercial basis. Over the years, the priority the Macri government gave to media regulation decreased, and the topic slipped off the political agenda at the end of his mandate (Califano, 2019). In those years, however, the number of new-born Indigenous broadcasters in the country reduced along with the financial support, infrastructure and frequencies assigned to existing ones (Riccap, 2019).

The Research

Design and Implementation

At the time I started my research, the situation of Indigenous media in Argentina was in a kind of limbo between legislation in the process of being dismantled but still in force (the LSCA) and other legislation planned but not formalised (the convergence-based one).

With regard to Indigenous media in particular, the scenario was as follows. The National Register of Indigenous Communities managed by the INAI counted 39 Indigenous nationalities, distributed among over 1600 communities throughout the country. In the North-West there is the greatest concentration of communities of diverse Indigenous peoples, mainly Andean ones (with the Kolla, the Diaguita-Calchaquí, the Lule-Vilela and the Guaraní being the most populous), while the North-East mostly contains the Pilagá, the Qom and the Mocoví. The latter are also found in the Centre of the country, mainly in urban or semi-urban areas, together with the Comechingón Sanavirón communities. The South, on the other hand, is occupied by the Mapuche and the Tehuelche, while some Huarpe communities persist in the Cuyo region. The Buenos Aires region gathers different Indigenous communities (mainly, Mapuche, Qom, Guaraní and Kolla peoples) forcibly translocated from their original areas after the dismantling of the Jesuit missions in the North and the military campaigns in the south (for a comprehensive overview of the geographical distribution of Indigenous people in Argentina, see the dossiers edited by the *Argentina Ministerio de Educación y Deportes*, 2016). According to official data provided to me in April 2016 by ENACOM and the *Defensoria del Público* (an authority established by the LSCA to defend audience rights), only 64 Indigenous communities were authorised to broadcast at that time, mostly in the North-West (34). Thirteen more were authorised in Patagonia, seven in the North-East, five in the province of Buenos Aires, four in the centre and one in Cuyo. As Riccap (2019) summarises, the concrete recognition of Indigenous media was neither systematic nor smooth under the LSCA. As for FOMECA, the diagnosis by Espada (2016) revealed that up to December 2015, only 90 of the 1013 concessions were assigned to Indigenous communities. Since 2016, fewer and fewer media have applied to the FOMECA competition and even fewer have received funding (Riccap, 2019).

Despite its weak application, the LSCA regulatory framework was remarkable for the percentage of the radio spectrum it reserved for non-profit organisations (33%), the founding human rights' doctrine on which it was based, the limitations it imposed on media concentration, and the participatory law-making process behind it (Marino, Mastrini & Becerra, 2011). Even more remarkable it appeared at the end of President Macri's mandate, which slowed down the mechanisms for financing and allocating frequencies. Moreover, the LSCA was pioneering in Latin America in recognising audio-visual communication service providers that had been invisible until then and in paving the way for implementing similar reforms throughout the region.[3] I refer to the Chilean Law 20.433 on Community and Citizen Broadcasting Services, enacted in 2010, that recognises both Indigenous peoples and non-profit organisations as licensees of such services (albeit with a limited power and within a regulatory framework that makes broadcasting unsustainable, Salazar 2014), the Colombian 2009 Law 1341 in which Indigenous media are included within the Sound Broadcasting Service of Public Interest as territorial broadcasters (Doyle, 2015a) and, above all, the 2011 Bolivian and 2013 Ecuadorian reforms mentioned in the Introduction, which directed me to Argentina.

Between 2016 and 2017, I carried out qualitative research aimed at exploring Indigenous media practices and characterising Indigenous broadcasters in order to understand their current situation from an emic perspective and support their calls for a more extensive and solid implementation of the LSCA. To do that, I interviewed Indigenous spokespersons (both women and men, young and older people[4]) from 34 out of the 64 communities that already had authorisation to broadcast, seeking the largest number of communities belonging to the different Indigenous peoples in each Argentinian region. I reached more than half of the communities that were authorised at the time, according to a purposive sampling strategy that ended up being evenly representative and proportionate (see Table 1.1). Of these, less than half were active and on air, but the authorisation, in establishing a medium, still constituted a sufficient milestone for exploring the genesis and objectives of the communication projects, their programming and agenda and their external relationships and internal organisation (with a focus on sustainability strategies). It also allowed respondents to express their opinions about the application of the LSCA and its media classification (having dealt with it since the authorisation process) as well as provide their own definition of 'community media,' 'Indigenous media' and 'communication with identity.' These stimuli, around which I structured the interview outline, favoured a variety of responses that I then coded both deductively and inductively for thematic analysis (Guest et al., 2011). This is how I identified the three semantic axes of Indigenous media activism mentioned in the Introduction and at the core of this book: the cultural and political matrix; the defensive and proactive attitude; and the outward and inward direction.

Table 1.1 List of Indigenous media considered in the research

Broadcaster	Indigenous people	Country region
FM El Puerto	Huarpe	Cuyo
Wall Kintun TV	Mapuche	Patagonia
FM Truwvliñ To Kom		
FM Akukiche		Buenos Aires
FM Nahuel Payun		
FM Aim Mokoilek	Mocoví	Centre
FM La Voz de los Pueblos		
FM Inti Puka	Comechingón Sanavirón	
FM Qadhuoqte	Qom	
FM Viquen		North-East
FM Lqataxac Nam Qompi		
FM Potae Napocna Navogoh		
Unnamed (FM 107.3)	Mbyá Guaraní	
FM Comunidad	Guaraní	North-West
FM Ñandereco		
FM Quarahy		
FM Monte	Lule Vilela	
FM Paj Sachama		
FM Sacha Hukup		
FM Raíces	Diaguita Calchaquí	
FM Libertad		
FM Ambrosio Casimiro		
FM Itay Kaimen		
FM Ruinas de Tinti		
FM Mukarra		
FM Identidad		
FM Ocan	Kolla	
FM Runa Simi Kolla		
FM Pachakuti		
Unnamed (FM 90.7)		
FM Whipala	Ocloya	
FM EL Antigal	Tilián	
FM Suri Manta	Sanavirón	
FM Maimará	Maymaras	

Epistemic Stance

I approached this work as a white, female researcher and activist from the Global North hoping to use my resources and skills to support struggles for Indigenous self-determination. I conceived and carried out this research as being engaged with issues of power and justice, according to a 'transformative paradigm' (Mertens, 2007), which allowed for honouring the Indigenous emic perspective on the research. I attempted to cross-pollinate the different areas of knowledge in play (Held, 2019) while accompanying Indigenous claims from the standpoint of solidarity and service, aware that even non-Indigenous researchers may contribute to the decolonisation project (Krusz, Davey, Wigginton, & Hall, 2020). As Tuhiwai-Smith (2016: 171) clarifies, knowledge production "expands and improves the conditions for [social] justice" as an "intellectual, cognitive and moral project, often fraught, never complete but worthwhile." This approach does not make my work a proper theoretical contribution to communication for social change generated from local theory as a point of engagement (Dutta & Pal, 2020) but represents an attempt at dialogue between theories and Indigenous praxes. A tangible example of this can be found in the way I adjusted my methods along the way and let the interviews become spontaneously collective when some media teams (responsible for managing the broadcasters) participated in their entirety. They not only appropriated and re-signified the moment but also the very data collection technique, according to the Indigenous practice of collectivising personal experiences (Wilson, 2001). On other occasions, the fieldwork itself became an opportunity to reciprocate through informal chats or live radio interviews, in which I shared updates about the study and exchanged preliminary analytical insights with Indigenous spokespersons, according to the Indigenous principles of co-constructing knowledge.

These research practices placed me in an interstitial position, consistent with my liminal experiences as a researcher and activist straddling the Indigenous and non-Indigenous world (Chawla & Atay, 2018). In this, I agree with Kovach (2009) when arguing for the importance of introducing ourselves in our writing and reporting: positionality affects the approach to the research itself. I experienced Indigenous media practices while living between the academy, alternative media and grassroots movements. I have moved back-and-forth through these three worlds and positioned myself as a 'researcher at the margins' (Tuhiwai-Smith, 2016), thus dealing with the tensions between academia and a commitment to social and cognitive justice. Tuhiwai-Smith herself suggests that those working at the margins need to adopt strategies to "do good research, to be active in building community capacities, to maintain their integrity, manage community expectations of them, and mediate their different relationships" (p. 170). In my case, this meant paying attention to the integrity of the research and people involved in it, alongside cultural sensitivity and an ongoing exercise of self-reflexivity and epistemic vigilance towards my research practices. The reactions of the Indigenous interlocutors and the way they perceived me drove me in this challenge. While some of them refused to participate, others did so with disappointment (they argued that it was not up to a non-Indigenous researcher to investigate or accompany Indigenous claims). These reactions were more than understandable in the light of the 'unethical research practices' that some scholars have applied in the field of Indigenous studies for a long time (Kovach, 2009). Besides being 'over-researched and othered' (Gerlach, 2018), Indigenous communities have been often studied through extractivist protocols that collect from the field but do not return to communities (i.e., the 'rape model' of research denounced by Datta, 2018). This feedback obliged me to unlearn my privileges and humbly rethink my role, stressing the collaborative dimensions of my research and taking responsibility for the participants (Datta, 2018).

This meant positioning myself within the research relationships and practices in a more genuine and appropriate way (i.e., the 'showing one's face' approach suggested by Tuhiwai-Smith, 2016), by inhabiting human relationships rather than professional ones and getting to know people rather than interviewing participants. I wanted to learn from Indigenous communicators rather than about them. Therefore, I re-framed my work accordingly along the way, although it was not always successful since the academic modes and times of knowledge-building imbued my research practices. I had to acknowledge, examine and try to dismantle my individual enmeshment within the colonial systems in an unfinished process of 'decolonising the self' (Lewis, 2018) that entailed an 'ever-present sense of discomfort' (Krusz et al., 2020) due to the ungrounded and inexperienced knowledge of the reality I approached. I had to recognise that I did not really understand what being-Indigenous and suffering physical and cultural subjugation for over 520 years really meant. In this, participating in the coeval #NiUnaMenos movement helped me, since the reflections and debates we had between female comrades of the National Network of Alternative Media of Argentina (RNMA) made me realise that our male companions could not fully understand the experience of patriarchal violence on women's bodies nor the power of the movement we were promoting. Then I realised that something similar applied to the colonial violence against Indigenous communities. Only then could I move away from the patronising assumption that researchers are expert knowers (Kovach, 2009) and the paternalistic conception that all activists are companions in the same struggle (Krusz et al., 2020); rather, I had to humbly listen and amplify the echo of what Indigenous people were and are still shouting from their media.

However, I did not *serve* the Indigenous cause as much, nor as well as I wanted to due to the professional and personal constraints which kept me in check and impeded the individual implementation of the 'bridgework' proposed by Ryan (2005). I navigated within the constraints of the community of scholarly resisters, leaning my weight on the side of solidarity. But by myself I was not able to open institutional and/or collective spaces for meeting and discussing the research results and, from there, understanding its practical usability. Nonetheless, I adopted a two-version strategy of scholarship dissemination, one for the activist audience and one for consumption by colleagues (Croteau, 2005), in which I uneasily negotiated between prioritising activism or an academic career as a scholar-activist. In this difficult operation, some Indigenous friends helped me by clarifying what they thought my study would contribute to. A Mapuche and a Kolla friend told me that they did not have enough time or resources to map the Indigenous broadcasters scattered around the country, or to list their problems, since they had other more pressing tasks and struggles to carry out; thus, in their view, my work was useful because I could go where they could not. Another Mapuche friend told me that she would use my report with the authorities to support the community's claims for liberating the radio frequency (unduly occupied by a local commercial radio station); in this way, an empirically based endorsement was useful to some extent. On the other hand, I shared the report with the team of the *Defensoria del Público*, which provides Indigenous communities and social organisations with legal assistance and technical training; I hope it helped to plan interventions and improve the broadcasters' conditions. In the meantime, scientific analyses circulate at conferences, in journals and books; in this way, I hope I have fed and added to a branch of studies too often marginalised in the academy. This book represents a further attempt to contribute to a report on both the Indigenous world I came to know through the research and what I learnt about how to approach and experience it.

Notes

1. The main Indigenous networks active in Argentina in the field of communication and other human rights of Indigenous peoples are the *Coordinadora de Comunicación Audiovisual Indígena de Argentina (CCAIA)*, the *Encuentro de Organizaciones de Pueblos Originarios (ENOTPO)*, the *Consejo Plurinacional Indígena* and the *Organización de Naciones y Pueblos Indígenas en Argentina (ONPIA)*. Each network brings together Indigenous peoples and organisations from different areas of the country and differs from the others in its political strategies and positioning (e.g., alliances with international agencies, NGOs and grassroots organisations, relationship with public policies and state regulations, relationship with regional and international Indigenous networks).
2. The LSCA also ensured that national audiovisual programming (including advertisements and programme previews) was expressed in native languages. In addition, it reserved for Indigenous peoples one AM, one FM and one television frequency in the localities where each people was settled. Finally, it recognised their right to have their own representative in some of the public bodies in charge of providing support in the application of the LSCA itself.
3. It is worth mentioning that in 2004, Venezuela had already approved the Law on Social Responsibility in Radio and TV, which included the participation of a representative of the Indigenous peoples in the Council that advised on the application of the Law, as well as the official character of Indigenous languages in mass media broadcasts. This regulation is an important legal antecedent in understanding the scope of the LSCA in that, although it took the first steps towards the recognition of Indigenous voices in the field of mediated communication, it did not grant them the right to manage their own media.
4. I do not reveal the identity of the Indigenous interviewees in accordance with the ethical protocol I applied throughout the research project, ruled by anonymity and data privacy informing the participants' consent. In reporting their responses in the following chapters, I shall therefore refer to their Indigenous nationality and/or their broadcasters only.

2   Territorial Struggles and the Media 'Weapon'

In Argentina, Amnesty International (2017) has identified over 300 territorial conflicts, most of which involve Indigenous communities defending their lands from dispossession and legal and environmental attacks, with the Northern and Southern regions reporting the highest number of controversial situations and even state-authorised violent repression. In the North-West, the dispute mainly involves the extraction of lithium and other mineral resources by multinational mining companies. In the province of Catamarca, for instance, Indigenous communities are fighting against large-scale mining projects known as the 'Mining Belt of Fire,' while in Jujuy the protests are about the extraction and export of lithium in the Salinas Grandes area. Additionally, deforestation and forestry exploitation jeopardise the balance of the communities, with environmental ramifications caused by pollution. In Santiago del Estero, for example, in 2015 the *Movimiento Campesino de Santiago del Estero – Vía Campesina* (MOCASE-VC), which includes many Lule Vilela communities along with the peasantry, mobilised in defence of families evicted by the soda company Manaus, which began clearing land and producing coal in the area. In the North-East also, extractive projects and deforestation, along with the expansion of large-scale production of soy, corn, wheat and livestock, are reconfiguring the regional agricultural production of cotton and increasing land ownership concentration. Legal issues are not lacking either. In 1998 the Wichí communities of Lahka Honat in Chaco appealed to the Inter-American Commission on Human Rights to protect their collective ownership and traditional use of their lands against the mega infrastructures planned by local government. Furthermore, the Qom communities in Formosa, well-known for camping out in Buenos Aires in 2015 under the leadership of Félix Díaz, engaged in a longstanding defence of their lands against the construction projects promoted by provincial government. The Mapuche people living in Patagonia, in contrast, mainly suffer from fracking and mining activities. The 'Vaca Muerta Shale' megaproject of Repsol-YPF and Tecpetrol in the Neuquén Basin, based on the exploitation

DOI: 10.4324/9781003243083-3

of hydrocarbons and the extraction of fossil fuels, is devastating the local economy and socio-cultural dynamics. The project has been developed in violation of the Indigenous peoples' right to free, prior and informed consent (guaranteed by the UN Declaration on the Rights of Indigenous Peoples and International Labour Organisation Convention 169) and foreshadows a significant increase in greenhouse gas emissions (thus undermining the objectives of the Paris Climate Agreement). As if that were not enough, Mapuche communities also continue to fight the Italian company Benetton, which owns and exploits 900,000 hectares of land in their ancestral territories and disavows their existence in word and deed. For that matter, the notorious disappearance and death of Santiago Maldonado in 2017 happened in the wake of the mobilisations in support of the Pu Lof community (in the province of Chubut) against the local activities of the Benetton Group. In Cuyo as well, most conflicts refer to private parties that acquire lands and forcefully evict the inhabitant communities, whereas in the centre of the country and in the Buenos Aires region Indigenous communities mainly face privatisation, gentrification, legal status issues and environmental problems, mainly derived from soy monoculture, fumigation and water pollution.

Throughout the country, therefore, the state apparatuses collude with the interests of large and small private companies that, in the name of progress and economic growth, undermine the local Indigenous communities both in their material and spiritual livelihood. I deliberately refer to these two dimensions because territorial conflicts exceed the physical dispute over the land and natural resources and rather imply what de la Cadena (2015) defines as an 'ontological clash' between opposing worldviews: the Indigenous and the colonial. The epistemologies of the North (Santos, 2018), on which global coloniality perpetrated by extractive companies and governments is based, approach territory merely as a geographical space with resources to be exploited. Conversely, the Indigenous conception of territory refers to an intrinsic and vital relationality between all living beings. In this respect, de la Cadena (2015) defines it as an entity that emerges through the Indigenous lifeforms and springs to life within the kinship relations and conversations between people and nature. It is a condition that transcends the mixing of humans and nature (because it makes each element more than just itself individually) and that emerges from a relationship that intrinsically connects all the elements (ibid.). Indigenous communities, especially Andean ones, centre life around the *Pachamama*, a sacred and dynamic living system formed by the indivisible community of all life systems and living beings (Gutiérrez-Chong, 2007). The Bill of Rights of Mother Earth, approved in Bolivia in 2010, states that humans and nature are interrelated, interdependent and complementary and work as a functional unit that inherently regulates the Indigenous lifeforms.

Such an ontological clash between conceptions and livelihoods precipitates in the ontic sphere, i.e., in the physical and spiritual encounter between Indigenous peoples and the West/North; this makes territory the perfect field in which to investigate the mechanisms of decoloniality at work. As Trerè and Pleyers (2015: 3816) state, the actual contribution of Indigenous struggles is that, when defending territories against governments that are exporting "commodities and food . . . into global markets" or against "land-grabbing, mining, and other extractivist industries," Indigenous peoples are not just protesting but also proposing "alternative worldviews and values, and implementing emancipatory perspectives" based on local autonomy and horizontal processes. Therefore, what is really at stake in the defence of land (the protest side of decoloniality, following Walsh, 2018) is the preservation and promotion of what the territory is in the Indigenous cosmogony and the alternative worldviews it implies (the prospect side).

However, the ontic clash with the West/North also underlies some safeguarding mechanisms and hybridisation processes that take place within Indigenous communities in the confrontation with the current settings of modernity and the contemporary forces of coloniality. For example, the dispute over the legal recognition of collective ownership of land (such as the one made by the Wichí communities of Lahka Honat in the Chaco) becomes a battleground for naming and conceptualising the relationship with land and the 'earth-beings' inhabiting it (de la Cadena, 2015) that would otherwise find no place in the vocabularies and entitlements of the state apparatus. Disputes against fracking (e.g., by the Mapuche against 'Vaca Muerta') resort to the anti-extractivist movements' vocabularies and the international regulatory framework to preserve the Wallmapu (the ancestral Mapuche nation straddling southern Chile and Argentina) from the devastation, which, per se, would not be understandable to environmentalist movements or international institutions. On the other hand, the Zapatista dictum 'a world where many worlds fit' attempts to challenge such homogenising effects of globalisation's universalism, proposing a transition towards what Escobar (2015) calls the 'pluriverse,' that is, the co-existence of different lifeforms without one suppressing or dominating the other. Whatever the approach or objective (to translate, negotiate and hybridise or preserve and coexist in differences), Indigenous territorial 're-existence' (Albán, 2013) is all about making room for Indigenous conceptions and practices of relating to the Earth and other living beings *against, beyond or within* the constraints imposed by the colonial world.

In these dynamics, the media play a pivotal role in that they stage, in sounds and images, in formats and nomenclatures, what Indigenous political worlding might otherwise fail to express to an outside society unable to understand other ontologies and informed by other values. As Nakata (2013: 130) states, "where there is a will to survive as distinct people who have the longest claim to the land, there will need to be language enough to describe continuity and persistence of distinctiveness in contemporary and future contexts." This is what the final declaration of the First Summit of Indigenous Communication of Abya Yala (2010) appears to refer to when stating that "Indigenous communication only has meaning if . . . it is at the service of life to make the struggles for our territories, for our rights, for our dignity and integrity known." What gives meaning and purpose to the media is 'making known,' in that it enables all that the territory represents for Indigenous communities, namely their physical and spiritual livelihoods, to be preserved and dignified. Indigenous media "exist because there is a strong reality that grounds the necessity for communicating this reality" (Salazar, 2003: 24). While denouncing the tears suffered by the territory, Indigenous media repair the inherent bonds within it; while narrating what happens, they create alternative scenarios.

In this chapter, I unpack the media practices supporting this territorial struggle of Indigenous peoples in Argentina: media practitioners fight in and for the territory, denouncing the violence of land dispossession and environmental damage while promoting an alternative model of the relationship between humankind and nature. I account for how Indigenous media practitioners *narrate* what happens in the territory, how they *stay in* it and finally how they *incorporate* the territory as a cosmogony into the media.

Calling to Action and Networking the Struggles

In his journey among grassroots radio experiences from different areas, Ramos-Rodríguez (2020) saw that Indigenous radio stations are an effective "tool in the resistance against extractive industries like mining or large-scale tourism . . . that threaten Indigenous territories" (p. 122). His words resonate in what different Indigenous spokespeople in the North-West told me when we met. The Diaguita Calchaquí manager of FM Mukarra, for instance, described their radio as "an important tool [in] the fight against mega mining." The Lule Vilela radio-makers referred to their FM Monte as "something they need for the defence of the territory [against] businessmen [who] take you away like a goat!" The FM Ocan's coordinator added that in the Kolla vision, media have to do "with the outward conflict against the provincial [and] national government, and . . . the farm owners." In other words, in an area like the Argentinian North-West, which is so diverse in terms of Indigenous nationalities and types of territorial conflicts, most Indigenous representatives describe the broadcasters as the slingshots in David's hands (Indigenous re-existence) against the giant Goliath (coloniality and its forces).

The first evidence where Indigenous media practitioners see the effectiveness of media as a 'defensive weapon' is that broadcasting widens the scope of the protests. According to them, providing local land-related protests with media coverage gives concrete support to the territorial struggle in that it motivates more people (mostly neighbouring communities and local citizens) to join the actions. In this regard, what the media practitioners of FM Maimará experienced is exemplary. They broadcast in the *Quebrada de Humahuaca*, a wide valley in the province of Jujuy declared a World Heritage and Biosphere Reserve by UNESCO and famous to international tourism for its colourful mountains and the Andean fauna and flora. There the difficulties of an arid mountain region are compounded by the consequences of a mass tourism that disregards local dynamics. When reporting from the radio (when it was active) on the roadblocks protesting for access to water or against the illegal usurpation of their lands, the Maymaras speakers had the feeling that they were "installing a critical gaze on these issues" in their audiences. They recalled receiving supportive phone calls and SMS of awareness-raising, thereby confirming that radio broadcasting could trace a sort of 'fighting horizon' within and beyond Indigenous communities. Moreover, one of them told me that when, a few years ago, cardon (a plant found in the North-West) was going extinct because "there was a lot of looting to sell the wood," the radio practitioners "began to denounce" this situation by publicly naming the culprits. As a result, people living in the area started to report the vehicles that were carrying cardon away when they saw them. In her view, "in this way also the radio [contributed to] preserving this plant" because it had a tangible effect on limiting cardon looting.

This case is emblematic of how a radio practice such as an announcement (i.e., 'media-as-practice,' Mattoni, 2020) might become a grassroots practice per se (i.e., 'media-in-practice,' ibid.) when replicating a typical political practice such as the *escrache* (a protest against a single person normally taking place in a public place to overtly discredit them) in communication technologies. Moreover, the Maymaras situations show that radio broadcasting not only works as a discursive device that can chart the horizons of a struggle but that it also has the performative capacity to activate solidarity responses on the factual level. This double effect particularly emerges from the words of the FM Pachakuti's coordinator: he perceived that they, as media practitioners covering land-related conflicts, were "strengthening the Indigenous movement, while making . . . its problems . . . visible." The Diaguita Calchaquí media-makers of FM Ambrosio Casimiro commented similarly: the radio station "communicates first-hand what is happening in the territory" and in doing so, contributes to "organisational strengthening." This is something Salazar (2003, 2014) saw in the self-representation practices mediated by the Mapuche online press agencies and here is enhanced by the communal cohesive dynamics typically promoted by the radio through the announcements service (Ramos-Rodríguez, 2016, 2020). I found examples of this also in the Kolla radio station FM Ocan in northern Salta, which regularly informs all the communities that constitute the Organisation of Aboriginal Communities of Nazareno (OCAN) about the administrative measures taken to regularise communal land ownership. The radio-makers saw this service as embedded in their struggle for ancestral land recognition given that confrontation with the state "also takes place within the bureaucratic procedures." The inner system of radio announcements is, therefore, politically re-signified.

A further way in which media provides Indigenous media practitioners with effective weapons for territorial struggles is the networking of Indigenous claims. They share information about what is happening in different ancestral lands and thereby join forces against similar domination mechanisms deployed by the state and/or private companies against Indigenous communities throughout the country. Indigenous media practitioners overcome and challenge the borders imposed by the state and redefine them by the logic of siblinghood and a sense of belonging to a common struggle. The Kolla FM Pachakuti radio station operating in Abrapampa (Jujuy), for example, broadcasts news about "the dispossessions, environmental problems, . . . and the clearances [happening] in Volcán, . . . Casa Grande . . . and Humahuaca" (i.e., throughout the province). On the Guaraní radio FM Quarahy, the news programmes report "the problems suffered . . . by Indigenous peoples of the whole North" (where the Guaraní people originally lived); the Mapuche radio FM Nahuel Payun is "twinned with the claims" of the Mapuche communities in Patagonia "against land usurpation and violation." Members of the Mapuche channel Wall Kintun TV even feel "obliged to broadcast content from other communities" as the only Indigenous television channel. Under authorisation, they transmit Qom and Diaguita documentaries sent by communities that have nowhere to broadcast them. Moreover, through Facebook, mail and face-to-face meetings, a single reporter collects information from different communities throughout the country, creating alliances with journalists of the radio stations that operate there. This is what makes him, in the words of the TV channel's coordinator, "a sponge" absorbing first-hand information everywhere and then releasing it in the channel news. Especially at demonstrations and protests, he only works with information coming from the communities: this was an editorial choice of the team, based on the fact that such information would have no room in the mainstream media that reproduces official or police reports and thereby criminalises the Indigenous struggles.

The Indigenous newsmakers' perception is that covering aggressions suffered by Indigenous communities in other areas based on reliable first-hand sources is akin to being on the spot and reporting from within. Indigenous media practitioners twin information agendas in the same way they twin their struggles. The Spanish term *hermanar* indicates precisely how what unites Indigenous peoples, namely, the trajectory of re-existence from a past and a present of usurpation and violence, is translated into a media practice per se. Depending on the context and urgencies, this might even be a goal in the agenda of the broadcasters, as is the case of the Mapuche radio station FM Nahuel Payun broadcasting in the Buenos Aires region. According to the coordinator, this is a very peculiar context in that it is inhabited by few Indigenous communities but of different peoples, as a consequence of displacements firstly from the 17th-century Jesuit missions in the north and later from the 19th-century military Conquest of the Desert in the south. He feels that this common experience of displacement should motivate communities to react together, with the media being the new battleground for experimenting with this siblinghood: "politics and religion have done us a lot of damage, they have fragmented us, . . . but now there are other means of conquest, the private and the governmental media, which are killing us little by little." In his view, responding together to these attacks through the media is a political practice per se that allows Indigenous communities to reconstitute what the conquests have damaged. As Ginsburg (1994: 378) states, "social relations built out of Indigenous media practices are helping to develop support and sensibilities for Indigenous actions for self-determination."

In all these stories I realised that the media are imbued with an ideology of dispute, already highlighted by Salazar and Córdova (2008) in proposing to see Indigenous videos as 'imperfect media.' The practical understanding of media as a weapon conceals a political conception of 'making known'; this intimately binds self-representation as a cultural process to the path towards self-determination as a political goal (Tuhiwai-Smith, 1999). Media are both discursive and performative artefacts that construct a reality while mediating it, thus working as an additional mediated form of political activism for cultural recognition (Salazar & Córdova, 2019). Indigenous media practitioners themselves took time to become aware of this. I remember, for example, that the Mapuche coordinator of FM Truwvliñ To Kom was initially sceptical about the concrete contribution of media to the territorial struggle. She was actively engaged in the territory and discussed local issues with her neighbours and siblings whilst considering what the media said as unimportant. Around her, "everyone was talking about communication," but for her it merited little attention because "there were a lot of things more important to talk about: for example, the animals dying because of drought." Eventually, she realised that material problems "have a common transcendent root." She told me: "Of course, if I never go out to take the floor and impart my reality, if I don't sit down to talk, there is no media that transmits [it]; and if we, the Indigenous people, cannot transmit our reality with our voices, nobody does." For her, that was a real paradigm shift in that self-representation became a constitutive part of the self-determination process contested in the field. Speaking on the radio became part of the 'continuum of representations' of the Mapuche reality (Salazar & Córdova, 2019). She realised that the territorial problems could not be solved if the battle were fought in an invisible niche by herself and a few Indigenous activists alone. This was the common transcendent root that the interviewee spoke about. It was necessary to get out of the niche to build situated alternative narratives and chart broader horizons of struggle. She realised that sharing the Mapuche reality would be an extension of their collective empowerment (Ginsburg, 1994) since media productions involve multiple actors, activities and arenas where Indigenous peoples can envision and create alternative scenarios to current realities while denouncing the existing ones. Broadening the scope of protests and intertwining the struggles are, therefore, tangible effects of self-representation as actual grassroots politics for the territory.

Being There and Acting Together

In reporting what happens in the territories, Indigenous media practitioners perform a further political practice that permeates Indigenous activism: direct testimony and, from this, the collective construction of alternative and situated versions of territorial conflicts. Indigenous media practitioners recover the Indigenous cultural tradition of first-person collective narratives, anchored in the materiality of bodies and territories, and translate them in the media into a statement of political position. This practice encapsulates both a decolonial critique of mainstream media (for their silence or misinformation about territorial conflicts) and a decolonial proposition of alternative ways of 'doing media' and fighting. Insights into this came to me when I spoke with a Lule Vilela spokesperson from FM Sacha Hukup in Monte Quemado (a province of Santiago del Estero) where the radio station is located. In 2011 Cristian Ferreyra, a young militant of the MOCASE-VC movement, was murdered for defending the 2,000 hectares of the Lule Vilela community to which he belonged from the soy businessman Jorge Ciccioli, who had already fenced off and begun clearing the land under authorisation by the provincial forestry department. A group of hired assassins appeared on a motorbike with guns at the house of Cristian's comrade Darío Godoy and shot the two boys, fatally wounding Cristian. The spokesperson of FM Sacha Hukup noted the fact that "other media did not" tell anything about this case, but the community really needed to make it public and "reach other communities far away." This is how the radio station came about in the first place, going on air officially on the second anniversary of Cristian's murder. In the experience of the Lule Vilela community and the whole MOCASE-VC movement, the silence of the mainstream media was complicit in both the assassination and the attacks on the territories. Symmetrically, starting a radio to tell an otherwise invisible story belongs to the same struggle and resistance carried out in the territories. Tying the commemoration of Cristian's assassination to the radio launch represents all this, keeping the memory of his struggle alive and telling it from the places and through the voices of those who are still carrying it forward. Likewise, the Diaguita Calchaquí radio station FM Ambrosio Casimiro arose from the same need "to change the communication logic of the hegemonic media," which provide "lying and distorted news . . . and manipulate reality" by "building [their] own stories, from [their] own experiences, and transmitting that to others." In these words, I understood that breaking the silence or telling their own version of territorial conflicts is not just a communicative goal for Indigenous communicators but rather a political gesture (enacted by staying on the field and putting their body on the line) and a cultural proposal (materialised in the effort of fostering a situated first-hand and collective counter-narrative).

In this regard, the coordinator of FM Pachakuti strongly argued that Indigenous media are different from other media "for standing where the conflict develops . . . and alongside the people, in cases where commercial media would . . . reproduce everything [they find] on the Internet." The team of Wall Kintun TV agreed on that: they report "what the person says" without editing the content and have a vocation to be where "nobody else would be" to cover evictions and land-related conflicts that "are usually silenced." A concrete example of this was conveyed to me by the Diaguita Calchaquí representative of FM Mukarra. The whole radio team mobilised in Catamarca against the mega-projects in the 'Mining Belt of Fire' with other local and international organisations. She told me that they "went . . . to protest in front of the mining companies' headquarters" and "walked together in this path of defending Mother Earth, because in Catamarca they are blowing up the hills." The Mapuche radio FM Truwvliñ To Kom participated in the protests by the Santa Rosa Leleque Community (in the province of Chubut) when the court of Esquel agreed to the eviction of many families from their lands that had been bought by Benetton. Broadcasting about land protection meant, therefore, putting oneself on the line. Moving towards self-determination is a concrete path to walk and broadcast in the places they want to protect, deploying against the extractivist model.

I could concretely grasp the importance of 'being there' when a Diaguita Calchaquí spokesperson from FM Raíces told me the story of Javier Chocobar:

> In 2009 some landowners . . . wanted to exploit the rock slabs, [although] the judge [had put] a clause [on them], according to which nothing could be taken out. [. . .] The justice raised up this precautionary measure and . . . when these guys entered, they pushed a *comunero*, they hit him with the butt of the gun. He had a camera to take pictures and, through that, we captured the scene . . . There was a struggle . . . they

shot many times and [at the end] shot Javier, who fell down . . . and unfortunately died there, while defending the land . . . We use the radio for [transmitting] that, and also for explaining . . . what the community is, why it defends the territory.

It was clear to me that, in this story, the camera and the radio were embedded in the struggle both physically and symbolically: they served to fight against the exploitation of the rock slabs, the eviction of the community and the murder of one of its members. These media truly reported the story of the events from where they happened, while revealing and explaining why the community is fighting. This is where I really see what Cerbino (2018) called 'commitment,' thereby recovering the term used by the final declaration of the II Summit of Indigenous Communication of Abya Yala (2013) to define Indigenous communication. He refers to the shift from the intimate dimension of defence and preservation (serving the community) to the public dimension of struggle and promotion (committing for the community). By 'staying there,' Indigenous media reinforce the lines of decolonial re-existence (Albán, 2013; Walsh, 2018) the community deploy on the territory. After all, this is also what makes Indigenous communicators troublesome for their adversaries. As a member of FM Inti Puka states, if "a bulldozer appears, they are the first to mobilise and . . . do not mind giving their lives for the territory"; and if "you give them a microphone, they are dangerous." No wonder that, for such a concrete engagement, Indigenous media practitioners also pay unfortunate consequences. For instance, when FM Pachakuti covered news relating to the mining companies operating in Jujuy, its reporters were "hit with stones . . . received weird, almost mafia messages [and] were insulted." FM Sacha Hukup even suffered an attempted arson attack and, later, armed threats. These kinds of repercussions are equivalent to those often suffered by activists occupying the streets, camping in front of institutions or sabotaging big private companies' projects. Thus, media practitioners are perceived as activists whose media activities seamlessly equate with all other grassroot political practices.

The practice of being there, of engaging body and soul with the territory and the community that is characteristic of Indigenous media activism, is confirmed by the efforts that Indigenous communicators also invest in extra-media activities. They organise and participate in several activities that animate community life, thereby reinforcing the organic link between broadcasters and community while blurring the boundaries between what is media-related and what is not. Indigenous communication thus infiltrates the social and environmental fabric, just as Almendra (2010) describes, while media-makers integrate and enhance the broader array of activities related to the defence and promotion of the territory. In doing so, they put precisely 'in practice' (Mattoni, 2020) what communication has always been for Indigenous peoples: that is, "a set of practices and processes that . . . is constitutive of the Indigenous social subject and of its symbolic expressions" (Magallanes-Blanco, forthcoming).

I saw this aspect, for example, when several Indigenous communicators told me that they often set up meetings with surrounding communities and organisations to define common strategies for confronting water supply issues, the lack of ambulances, drug addiction and alcoholism among young people. They feel that it is their task to be involved in resolving these problems as they can enable a broad debate from which to establish a common position to be advanced to local institutions. I saw this call to 'do something together' in the radio-bingo that FM Potae Napocna Navogoh launched to raise funds and "buy toys or chocolate for the kids." Paying attention to younger people is understood as a constitutive part of Indigenous communication. As some Indigenous media practitioners in Oaxaca, Mexico recently stated (Collective Author, 2018), they have "a responsibility [to] take into account . . . childhood, adolescence, and youth, . . . by actively working within the new generations' education from an intergenerational standpoint." I also understood the political value of the participation of Lule Vilela media practitioners in the "camps, assemblies, and political training schools" organised by the MOCASE-VC. In these meetings, the movement works on its internal ethnic diversity (created by the participation of creole and Lule Vilela people) with formulas of *mestizaje* (i.e., the 'peasant-Indigenous' epithet by which the movement names itself) that challenge the historical 'de-indianisation' of the country's memory (Briones, 2003; Briones & Delrio, 2007). The Lule Vilela media practitioners, by participating in these meetings, absorb and embrace this mestizo identity self-ascription and then replicate it in radio activities to consolidate it within the movement while promoting it outwards in the public (mediated) sphere. I glimpsed the importance of corporeality in the efforts that communicators from FM Pachakuti spent in organising and then advertising the enactment of "the battle of *Colpayo* and . . . *Abra de la Cruz*" to commemorate and re-signify Indigenous participation in the achievement of Argentinian independence from the Spanish crown. This commitment to narrating the Indigenous world also materialises in editing books about Indigenous legends or teaching about traditional architectures and handicrafts in schools and libraries. Indigenous communication flows seamlessly between different supports and activities, as Almendra (2010) reveals, to weave Indigenous memory and knowledge as a further step towards self-determination (Tuhiwai-Smith, 1999). Likewise, supporting local economic activities is not just about advertising but also participating in the agricultural cooperatives "that process the *quinoa*" (FM Maimará, Maymaras) or selling "the *yacón* [and] the goat products, such as cheese and meats" directly at the radio stations (FM Whipala, Ocloya). These activities unfold seamlessly between broadcasters and food producers, with media formats (e.g., radio announcements) activating alternative buying and selling circuits with the potential to emancipate communities from the capitalist yoke. The praxeological understanding of communication, therefore, transcends the media while including them. It is inherent to the political and cultural (and even economic) significance that staying-there, making-visible and doing-together have in the Indigenous world. In this way, (mediated) communication becomes an inherent part of the territory itself.

Inhabiting the World Another Way

While fighting *for* and *in* the territories, Indigenous media practitioners end up incorporating the territory into the broadcasters. The osmosis between media and territory, the chain between making it known, being there and thus embedding it in the media, clearly emerged in an interview with the Diaguita Calchaquí representative of FM Identidad.

> The land-related issues are what we have always been *fighting for*, [it is about] *making* a little more *visible* to society, through the media, why we fight for the land, [i.e.,] not for our own or economic interests, but so that future generations will have a place to live. In our vision, *the land does not belong to us, but we belong to it*: that is the way we think culturally, that our ancestors have always promoted . . . First there is the defence of the land and then its development within the community, that is, the *development of the Buen Vivir and the care of nature* . . . to educate young people in different areas, such as health and education, [so that] they can then transfer this *knowledge* to the community itself.

In his words, the need to let the public know what is happening in the territory also implies the need to promote and develop what the territory is in the cultural life of the Indigenous communities. He refers to a relationship of mutual belonging to the Earth, from which knowledge and skills are released and circulate virtuously between territory and community. This underlies an Indigenous conception and practice of communication which springs from the territory itself and finds a natural habitat in the media.

Sometimes this incorporation is announced even in the name of the broadcasters as a sort of declaration of intent to position the radio in the territory, while bringing the latter into the former. For instance, FM Monte defends the nearby mountain from plundering and deforestation, and FM Mukarra commemorates the last Diaguita Calchaquí leader fighting against the Spanish conquest. Some names encapsulate the sacredness of the land, its spirituality. For instance, the Tilián radio station FM El Antigal mentions the ancestral archaeological site where the radio is based, while the Diaguita Calchaquí radio FM Ruina de Tinti honours the sacred ruins located in the area where the community lives. Other names refer to the local fauna and flora, and thus to the interdependence between humans and earth-beings that underpins community life. This is the case of FM Suri Manta that likens the radio to the *suri* (the local flightless bird that, according to Sanavirón Comechingón beliefs, protects the territory) or the Diaguita Calchaquí radio FM Raíces, which quotes the roots coming from the adobe of which the radio building is made. From their very name, all these stations show how the broadcasters are materially and symbolically part of the territory, positioning themselves in the media arena with the intention of making it clear from the outset that the rights of Mother Earth and the benefits of a sustainable environment are part of ethnic identity (self–)ascription and the exercise of Indigenous rights to communicate and share their identity.

All of this can also converge in radio programmes. As the Diaguita Calchaquí coordinator of FM Libertad explained, programmes "do not only deal with conflicts, [but also] with the good things that exist in our territories, such as the *Pachamama*, . . . because it is also a way of revaluing identity." There is a link between territory and Indigenous identity that justifies but also transcends the struggle for its defence, and the media are called upon to disseminate it. In this regard, the Mapuche coordinator of FM Akukiche explained to me that they "always talk about a *territorial identity* concept, which is contained by Mother Earth, and which encompasses everything." In her words, territory and identity merge in the same concept in that the former is conceived as "the physical, spiritual, symbolic, historical and cultural space where one belongs because one is part of it" (Magallanes-Blanco, forthcoming). Therefore, "living there means a co-responsibility and historical continuity," which is what substantiates the defence of the territory as an identity claim: giving up on it means giving up Indigenous history, culture and ancestry (ibid.). The Mapuche interviewee added that what they express on the radio "is pure *identity sensitivity*" since it "does not deal with material issues [but rather] with human issues that, however, transcend us." In her words, identity is a spiritual force encapsulated in the territory as a living habitat, within and around which Indigenous peoples shape their own project or resistance and revitalisation. Indigenous media practitioners support this project; while covering the attacks and dispossessions otherwise disregarded by mainstream media, they also convey the vitality and relationality reinvigorating the territory (de la Cadena, 2015), the spiritual dimensions that need to be protected just as much as material resources and which entail a proposition of being in the world in another way. This is what Whyte (2011) calls 'recognition justice,' a decolonial practice that consists of denouncing harm while promoting the value of "the socioecological contexts required for Indigenous populations to experience the world as a place infused with responsibilities to humans, nonhumans and ecosystems" (Whyte, 2016: 3). Decolonial resistance and empowerment overlap in the media because, while denouncing material attacks on land and nature, Indigenous communicators also speak of and promote their own 'other way' of inhabiting the world, with relatedness and siblinghood imbuing the territory. This is how Indigenous peoples recognise themselves inwardly and want to be recognised outwardly in Western/Northern society. The media are designed accordingly. The concept of 'Communication with Identity' (CCAIA, 2012) promoted by Indigenous organisations during the discussion of the LSCA has to do with this identity claim, aimed at cultural recognition and performed in the media as additional spaces/tools of the Indigenous struggle for self-determination.

Speaking with some Diaguita Calchaquí media practitioners, this interplay between territory, communication and decoloniality unfolding on the dual level of materiality (natural and human resources) and spirituality (human and earth-beings) became clear to me. Representatives from FM Raíces and FM Mukarra, for instance, explained that "the land is . . . the community itself": they perceive that they are "part of the earth," not just because they live there but because they "live off nature, off sowing and then harvesting to eat, off animals and medicinal herbs that are in the hills." In their words, I captured the material and spiritual bond they have with the territory as Diaguita Calchaquí people, as well as the commitment they feel to defend that bond as media practitioners. The role communication concretely plays in this bonding and engagement was not immediately clear, but when I talked with the coordinator of FM Itay Kaimen, I understood. He said that, for his people, "communication means understanding the relationship . . . between human beings, [and] also the relationship that humans experience as a part of that territory." The Diaguita Calchaquí, for instance, "communicate with the hills" because they are "connected" with them to the extent that they are able to "identify when it is going to rain, when it is going to be windy, . . . if the sowing has to be brought forward." In the territory, he said, "there is [this] deposit of knowledge handed down by the elders," which is imbued with sacredness. The members of the Qom radio station FM Lqataxac Nam Qompi told me something similar.

[Our] cosmovision [guides] how we see the world, how we identify, for example, the natural environment, how our ancestors had that spiritual feeling or that spiritual connection with natural beings. And [this] often translates . . . into radio. For example, if we tell a story, we use . . . the sound of nature more than anything else [because] our ancestors were guided by nature. From the sun, they were able to diagnose or predict many changes.

In these narratives, communication refers to what Escobar (2014) calls '*sentipensar*,' that is, conversing, feeling and thinking simultaneously with nature (e.g., the hills, the rain, the wind, the sowing, the sun), culture (e.g., the intergenerational knowledge transfer) and knowledge (e.g., the ability to connect with natural elements, the skills to recognise the signs of atmospheric phenomena). It is in this definition of communication as embedded in the sacredness and wisdom of the Earth that I realised how communication concretely reproduces the "systems of thought that expose forms of relationship between subjects and between subjects and the environment, both based on the valorisation of what is human and of nature" (Magallanes-Blanco, forthcoming). Communication exceeds the modern/hegemonic logics and subjects: just as Aguirre (2002) suggests, it rather flows amid all community members (including the ancestors who are repositories of knowledge and traditions) and interconnects them with earth-beings.

Indigenous media practitioners can restore this conception and practice of communication in media production and products, thereby also challenging in the media arena the Western/Northern conception of territory and related exploitative practices. They can discursively support such a different lifeform outwardly, but also perform it inwardly while returning communication to its original functions and dynamics. In this regard, the final declaration of the II Summit of Indigenous Communication of Abya Ayala (2013) states that "Indigenous communication is committed to the defence of life and . . . the struggle for land and territory, made up of subsoil, soil and airspace, all of which are conceived as sacred in our worldviews." Indigenous media practitioners are, therefore, called to a political/physical commitment (i.e., the defence of subsoil, soil and airspace by making known and standing there) stepping into Indigenous culture/symbolism (i.e., the defence of life and the sacred value of land by incorporating them in the media). They have the job of representing such an alternative ontology of territory, characterised by relatedness and mutuality between humans and non-humans (de la Cadena, 2015) while disputing the colonial one, characterised by exploitation and domination. As the representative of Wall Kintun TV told me at the end of the interview: "the function of the TV channel is to be the nexus between the air and the Indigenous communities, between the frequency and them." In her words, even being in the ether to transmit refers to this material and symbolic incorporation of the media in the territory in all its constitutive parts. Enabling the connection between community and territory is what communication, including mediated communication, does.

On FM Akukiche this connection was particularly evident in its cultural programmes, which convey the relationship with the Earth by means of Mapuche sounds and traditions. The coordinator told me that "you hear the background sound of the *Piflica*, the *Trutruca* or the *Trompe* (some Mapuche musical instruments)" and this "will give you [the perception] that you are talking to 'the people of the land, who speak in the wind.'" One of the programmes was called *Kurum Turvf Mapuche*, which means that, "and it speaks about the weather, how the sun came up, or what happened to the wind." It "began by talking about the language, with very nice phrases [in Mapudungun] about why [the Mapuche people] are in such a territory characterised by the wind." In her view, this served to "provide a sample of the essence of the territory," thereby conveying the spiritual meaning of the Mapuche territory in radio format and content.

Therefore, by performing the Indigenous 'way' of communicating in the media, Indigenous practitioners restore it and, at the same time, break into the media arena with the Indigenous 'way' of inhabiting the territory. This osmosis between inward restoration and outward challenge was particularly evident to me when I visited FM Ambrosio Casimiro. The radio programme named *Airampo* promotes "the ancestral forms of knowledge production and cooking, and mixes them with the Diaguita [Calchaquí] health." It gathers the results of community work, knowledge recovery and education on the native health and food, which is centred on Mother Earth's products and their value. I was able to sample this work when, during the radio visit, I was invited to one of the workshops on these issues. The attendees explained how to recognise the edible seeds of the sclerophyllous forest surrounding the community, indicating the therapeutic properties of each one of them as well as their culinary combinations. As Gutiérrez-Chong (2007: 319) states, "the recovery of ancient traditions takes place through direct interchange with nature." In this case it was also invested with a counter-hegemonic value, questioning Western/Northern food manufacturing and pharmaceuticals with an alternative culture of health and taste centred on the proximity of food products and the relevance of ancestral medical knowledge. The radio programme becomes a transmitter of this inward recovery of knowledge and interchange with Mother Earth. As the radio representatives explained, it tells of ancestral illnesses and healings and from there reconstructs the healing and nutritional properties of plants and seeds. Seamlessly, the *Airampo* programme and the workshop feed the Indigenous practice of promoting medicines and recipes as a cultural intervention that conveys the political demand to approach the humankind-nature relationship holistically. The radio programme allows this demand to be conveyed outwardly, in the media arena, where it explicitly challenges Western/Northern cooking and health by both presenting concrete cases in which medicinal plants and seeds can be used to cure (or even prevent) diseases that Western/Northern medicine usually treats with chemical drugs and by reviving traditional recipes using these plants and seeds in a holistic approach to health and nutrition often lost in Western/Northern lifestyles.

This alternation between Indigenous ontology and the Western/Northern categories is something that Magallanes-Blanco (2015) also found when analysing Indigenous videos as rhetorical tools to convey the relationship between Indigenous peoples and nature. In her study, simple images or intimate dialogues humanising nature or valuing interrelatedness in Indigenous videos represent the care-taking relationship between Indigenous peoples and Mother Earth, whereas legal discourses and non-Indigenous references mainly denounce land dispossession and environmental degradation. In my experience with Indigenous media in Argentina, this alternation of references is usually reflected in the whole programming, with cultural programmes conveying the Indigenous cosmovision anchored in the territory and information programmes denouncing land usurpation and claiming Indigenous rights, according to categories more familiar to non-Indigenous audiences. It is a useful practice to make the territorial dispute intelligible to a non-Indigenous audience and, thereby, bridge that ontological clash described by de la Cadena (2015) between the Indigenous and colonial ontologies of territory. In this way, a dispute over the cultural recognition of Indigenous identity springs from defence of the territory. It is placed at the juncture between the effort to recover and reinvent Indigenous beliefs, traditions and languages, and the questioning of cultural domination that has infiltrated Indigenous lifeforms. The media thus become spaces/tools for this cultural dispute, with Indigenous communication recovering its original meanings and acquiring new ones.

3 Cultural Contention and Media 'Enactment'

When I visited the Diaguita Calchaquí radio stations in the province of Salta, a member of FM Ambrosio Casimiro told me that, before founding the radio station, members from different Diaguita Calchaquí communities came together in a media training session to brainstorm what communication was for them. They realised that it consists of "the messages found in [the] engraved stones . . . the engravings on the pots, the smoke signals, and then the *Chaskis*, the *coplas*, the *bagualas* (typical Andean dances)." They were discussing a body of signals and formats that engages corporeality and sensoriality, thus implying contact between humans, as well as between humans and their surroundings. A few days later, this report resonated in the words of the coordinator of FM Itay Kaimen who said that the Diaguita Calchaquí people consider communication to be a "system" composed of "the paths, the shouts, the whistles, . . . the stories of experiences . . . told in first person." In his opinion, these elements turn communication into an actual "living actor" in that it "vitalises their culture, their identity and their organic forms of daily organisation." These descriptions reminded me of those threads in Almendra's (2010) conception of communication as a textile; those mechanisms connecting members and entities that oil organisational dynamics and lubricate the web of relationships within and between the Nasa communities of northern Colombia. I realised how far my idea of communication was from that of Indigenous peoples, where every sign, every object and being, and every experience acquires a spiritual meaning and communicates something. Communication reproduces Indigenous cosmogonies by working as a mechanism for "the collective production of meaning, the construction of the social, the establishment of consensus, norms and values, and identity links" (Magallanes-Blanco, forthcoming). I felt instantly catapulted into a different set of cultural and communicative practices and was able to measure the scope of the Indigenous communicators' decolonial challenge in the field of culture and knowledge-building. They must make room for the spiritual and relational experience that shapes community lifeforms, produced and

DOI: 10.4324/9781003243083-4

circulated through different languages and devices such as orality, icono-graphic representations, corporeal and sound arts or monuments (Beltrán, Herrera, Pinto, & Torrico, 2008). In this regard, Gutiérrez-Chong (2007) speaks about the 'vivid expressions of Indigeneity' to encompass all the cultural practices that substantiate Indigenous cosmogony. She mentions "symbolic codes of dress and adornment, social relations, domestic behaviour, gender roles, religious rituals, festivities and cults of nature, . . . literary production, language and music . . . [and] memory" (p. 315). This variety of codes, this vitality of languages and dynamics has to find readaptation in the media, where they materialised and are reinvented in order to affirm Indigenous culture outwardly whilst strengthening ethnic affiliation inwardly.

According to the Diaguita Calchaquí interviewees, transferring all of this to a radio format "was simply a matter of putting a microphone to the whole process" and "using some techniques." However, in this shift from the symbolic to the material, from cultural to media practices, I understood that there is more involved than simply technological translation. It is rather a matter of imbuing these cultural processes and (media) products with political positioning, mixing the propositional with the contentious through an interplay I recognised when I spoke with a Huarpe communicator from FM El Puerto. She considered the media as spaces for displaying political contestation rooted in Indigenous cultural performances that were otherwise supplanted by colonial ones:

> It is not a matter of [simply] being against capitalism or the church, but rather knowing where we come from. So, if we perform the ceremony to the god of rain who now has the name of a saint, we should know what we are doing! This conflicting aspect is what we should communicate.

In her opinion, media should empower Indigenous traditions and beliefs (the ceremony to the god of rain) by raising awareness about the cultural colonisation (the replacement with a ceremony for a saint) and denouncing its perpetrators (the capitalist system and the church). This sounded like it was opening up a creative symbolic arena both to locate Indigenous myths, memories and symbols and to use and combine Indigenous imagery with other types (in this case Catholic imagery) as a political stance. This provides a particular insight into the meaning of performing identity at the touchpoint between the Indigenous and non-Indigenous world, i.e., at the 'cultural interface' (Nakata, 2007) represented by the media. Indigenous cultural practices (e.g., rituals) are spurious in that they are products of the decolonial practice of retrieving, revitalising and legitimising indigeneity while coming to terms with the hegemonic culture. As the coordinator of Wall Kintun TV said, the function of the TV channel is precisely "to restore the value of the Mapuche cosmovision because many good things that the Mapuche people had have been extinguished, and thanks to a medium of communication they can be revived, be it in medicine, spirituality, cooking . . . everything!" The media, therefore, convey both the political meaning and historical trajectory of Indigenous cultural practices. According to Gutiérrez-Chong (2007: 313), media have the advantage of bringing the past, "a key concept in the definition and negotiation of [Indigenous] identity," into the present, thus posing "a problem for . . . the builders of the . . . state." This is where the self-determination process described by Tuhiwai-Smith (1999) takes on consistency: it is not limited to the survival of ancestral cultures; rather, it requires their recovery and development (while dealing with the cultural expressions and means of coloniality). These steps transform Indigenous cultural activism into an actual 're-existence' in the sense proposed by Albán (2013): performing ancestral rituals, retracing the origins of words, textiles or foods, and recounting legends and myths in radio or visual productions make media genuine devices for dignifying and re-inventing life within the reality established since colonialism. The Diaguita Calchaquí coordinator of FM Itay Kaimen synthesised this chain of processes when explaining the decision to schedule programmes dealing with what he called "cultural issues." These programmes more than others allow radio listeners to understand "where [the Diaguita Calchaquí] are positioned when talking, that is, [in their] pre-existence, beyond the state's recognition." In that 'beyond' I found the key: the state exists, and the history of cultural genocide perpetrated by the coloniality of power (which is opposed by the reference to 'pre-existence') is a constitutive part of the political re-signification and cultural enactment (through and in the media) of what being Indigenous means today. Indigenous media practitioners act out a 'cultural intervention' (Ginsburg, 2016) as a practice both of resistance to cultural hegemony and empowerment of ethnic recognition and self-determination. Media provide technological support for this cultural operation steeped in politics.

In this chapter, I examine the media practices involved in the recovery and revitalisation of those Indigenous traditions, languages and beliefs which convey political demands relating to the legitimacy of Indigenous knowledge and lifeforms, as well as to their resistance to hegemonic ones. Each section explores a specific expression of Indigenous activism in the battlefield of culture, acted out and re-signified in the media: firstly, the narration and oral transmission of knowledge and historical truths; secondly, the authenticity of communal relations and dynamics as an antidote to stereotypes; and finally, the use of native languages and openness to intercultural dialogue.

Hi-Storytelling and Intergenerational Transmission

The first sign of Indigenous cultural contention may be found in the very choice of the radio medium. It is no coincidence that there is only one

Indigenous television channel (Wall Kintun TV, Mapuche, Patagonia) in Argentina. Most communities have resorted to radio not only for practical reasons (i.e., greater economic sustainability, technological and organisational ease) but also for the cultural and political value that orality has in the Indigenous world. As Wilson (2015) points out, radio, more so than other media, translates the Indigenous practice of orality into media practice. In this regard, Ramos-Rodríguez (2020: 13) argues that radio allows for the transmitting of "the spoken or sung word" which is "the most important carrier of language, cultural values, and identity" of Indigenous populations. He refers to the oral word as "the raw material of radio" (ibid.); this is a compelling definition since it suggests that Indigenous radio practitioners then shape that raw material. When broadcasting, they enact (while recovering and revitalising) orality itself as a specific Indigenous cultural practice. That raw material acquires quite different meanings from those assigned by modern Westerners, for whom the oral word is not very trustworthy (*scripta manent verba volant*). This cultural opposition of values and sense-making became clear to me when I spoke with the Mapuche coordinator at FM Akukiche. She explained the meanings attached to the radio microphone:

> Today . . . whoever has a microphone has a gun in their hand . . . but we see it from another angle, because it is from another angle that we consider orality . . . that is, as a synonym . . . for the value of the truth of my word . . . That microphone must function as when we are standing around the stove or when we are in the *Wüñoy Tripantu* (celebration of the return of the sun) or in the *Traun* (assembly), where face-to-face . . . we do *kiñey rakiwuan* (discussion until reaching unanimity).

In these words, I came to recognise how the practice of speech is pivotal in the Indigenous world. It involves objects, rituals, people, places and knowledge both in cultural and political situations (such as celebrations and assemblies) informed by horizontality and circularity. Moreover, oral communication encapsulates a heuristic value (the value of the truth) that has nothing to do with the frequent abuse or misuse of oral words present in the mainstream media (as implied by her reference to the gun). This makes orality an actual claim to the right to a 'decolonial difference' (Mignolo, 2001). Speaking on the radio, as explained in the last excerpt, is a decolonial gesture in that it allows for the (re)production and appreciation of the cognitive value of Indigenous experiences and practices whilst revealing the coloniality of power from their own perspective. The 'other angle' from which the Mapuche people approach the microphone refers to this exercise of oral speech as a cultural enactment with a political value. The microphone conveys the centrality of the word, the circularity of storytelling, the truthfulness of lived experience, the condemnation of past or current events, and the proposal to live in the world differently.

In this regard, Rivera-Cusicanqui (2008) highlights that orality is an actual Indigenous historiographical practice which implies a collective reflection on the experience of subjects who have been oppressed by colonial power structures. It opens a circular and dialectic space in which to identify and understand the profound implications and tactics of the colonial order through the eyes and voices of subjugated peoples. This conception is deeply rooted in the founding plan of the Comechingón Sanavirón radio station FM Inti Puka. According to its members, "official history in Argentina distorted the truth" about Indigenous peoples, and they felt a strong responsibility "to [account] to the others how [their] people actually used to live," to reverse "such a process of colonisation that continues to this day." Oral hi-storytelling makes it possible to recover subjective experiences and to value them as an alternative to the official history and historiography that condemn the voices of the underdogs to silence. In this respect, the media practitioners of FM Libertad explained that, in the vision of the Diaguita Calchaquí people, the radio "is part of their voice" precisely in opposition to the fact that "they have always [been] silenced." Going on air means providing an oral counter-narrative to historiography:

> I read histories and historians, and . . . they say: "The Diaguita Calchaquí used to live here." That's a big lie: we still live here! . . . As we have always said: they have cut down the branch, the trunk, but they have not touched our roots, and today our voice is beginning to sprout, and they will never again [be able to] silence us.

Through radio the Diaguita Calchaquí communicators foster a cultural proposal that, in turn, refers to the collective way in which Indigenous peoples conceive and practice reporting activities. As Cerbino (2018) argues, Indigenous media practitioners "recover the function of telling reality in the first person and in a collective way, without the interference of intermediaries." This consideration is echoed in the responses of many interviewees. The communicators of FM Itay Kaimen and FM Lqataxac Nam Qompi, for instance, made this point explicit when declaring that they want to make the radio stations "a more trustworthy space," where Indigenous "brothers and sisters [can] give testimony" and construct a "new history" together, in opposition to the official, top-down one otherwise "embodied in the books." The intermediation of the radio replaces that of schoolbooks and thus guarantees situated information rooted in the stories of those who have experienced history in the first-person plural. These responses anchor the production of unknown and alternative knowledge to the broadcasters as a collective space for exchange to counter the never-ending history of violence and marginalisation that remains unofficial and invisible. In doing so, media sustain the practice of exercising what Soler (2017) calls the 'right to reply'; that is, to tell their own version of Spanish colonisation and state settlement up to the current evictions and displacements, and the impact of extractivism in their ancestral territories. They rewrite the past and the present through the direct witness of protagonists, thus sharing a sort of 'present history' (ibid.) along which coloniality has unfolded. In this regard, a member of FM El Puerto clarified that Indigenous radio is based on "knowing the history and knowing what position we have in the territories and what we have inherited." In other words, decoloniality materialises in the practice of communicating historical memory and present testimony through/in the media, along a collective narrative that mirrors Indigenous communality and embeds their lived and shared experiences. For this reason, oral narration is an inherent part of Indigenous activism: it is an exercise of collective memory through which "the past acquires new life as the central foundation of Indigenous cultural and political identity, and as a source of radical criticism of the . . . forms of oppression [exercised] on the Indigenous [peoples]" (Rivera-Cusicanqui, 2008: 166).

Passing on knowledge and lived experience from the oldest to the youngest is a constitutive part of this history-building operation carried out by Indigenous peoples through radio broadcasting. Oral traditions connect the past with the present in an attempt to exercise memory through an ideal transgenerational handover (Gutiérrez-Chong, 2007). The aforementioned founders of FM Inti Puka automatically linked the need to tell another history about Indigenous peoples with the need to tell it specifically to young people who had not experienced crucial moments in Indigenous peoples' trajectory and hence "cannot love what [they] do not know." Speeches and oral storytelling are not a "passive legacy of . . . past grievances" but rather a "cross-generational transmission of past injustices, transforming storytelling . . . into [a] critical site for motivating political mobilisation" (Farthing & Kohl, 2013: 364). In this regard, Ramos-Rodríguez (2016) specifies that such a trans-generational impact of Indigenous media encourages young people to reaffirm their ethnic affiliation and engage with Indigenous activism; this is why, for instance, the Huarpe radio-makers of FM El Puerto see the radio mainly as a tool for "keeping culture alive . . . by reaching the seed of some children." They understand radio activities as a cultural operation of orality restyling, informed by Indigenous values (i.e., inter-generationality) and modern formats, which might be catchy and more effective on the young. On the other hand, such activities also underlie a gesture of political opposition against a non-Indigenous society that casts off the exercise of speech while facilitating the fragmentation and dispersion of memory in intergenerational transition (Gutiérrez-Chong, 2007).

Here I understood a further element of the political significance that invests such cultural intervention: trans-generational cohesion. Strengthening the links between the young and older people through media not only resists losing the transfer of values and knowledge, it also suggests alternative ways of healing generational gaps. As Ramos-Rodríguez (2020: 126) explains, thousand-year-old Indigenous knowledge includes "information on plants, animals, spirituality, and Indigenous worldviews," which might not seem of interest to the younger generation; nonetheless, radio has allowed "documenting, archiving, digitising and transmitting such knowledge" to them (ibid.), thus strengthening inner community relationships. A Guarani leader from Misiones clearly illustrates how this transfer 'knots up' perfectly on the radio:

> Most of us are hunters or forest fruit collectors. Perhaps one thinks that the fishing system has nothing to do with the radio, but it does . . . because . . . when we have the radio on air, that story will be commented on, and young people will get to hear that story much better . . . Our storytelling system is based on language, so it is oral: . . . we have always passed on our customs, our way of life, orally, from generation to generation.

Orally transmitting habits and history through radio is a strategy for bridging generation gaps. Radio intercepts young people's attraction to communication technologies while updating older people's modes of expression. The same Guarani leader of Misiones explains that the elders of his community decided to establish a radio station in order to "capture the young people who are moving away" from the community and its values: the radio was to be "a meeting point" with them. In other words, it operates as a 'cultural interface' (Nakata, 2007) that hosts an intergenerational encounter in which a negotiation between traditional knowledge and formats (of which the elderly are the custodians and with which the young have to deal) and the languages and tools of the hegemonic culture (where the young are the drivers and the elderly novices) comes to the fore as a meeting across different age cohorts. Such an encounter ends up challenging the intergenerational relationship practices of our Western/Northern society while proposing another pattern of relationality that is based on listening and learning. In this respect, the team running FM Itay Kaimen was particularly instructive. Diaguita Calchaquí communicators explicitly blamed our Western/Northern attitude of dismissing elderly people and underestimating the young. They rather emphasise the intergenerational continuity that Indigenous sociability promotes and preserves:

> When non-Indigenous society says "Well, all the old people are dying and all the history is going away [with them]," [it] neglects our young people

and children who are . . . actually acquiring knowledge from our grand-parents. [Instead], we believe that [there is] continuity: even if our grand-parents must physically leave this space, they remain in each one of us.

In these words, knowledge transmission and memory are not just about cultural preservation but are concerned with adopting a different relational model. This means implementing social practices that strengthen ties based on a cultural practice that becomes a political alternative to our forms of life. This point was made even more clearly when Qom communicators from FM Potae Napocna Navogoh said they often interview the elderly to "speak about the ancestors" and "transmit their wisdom," or when I discovered that on FM Identidad the "old wise men" share their experience on a designated programme. In this regard, Tuhiwai-Smith (1999) highlights that the cultural activism of Indigenous people involves tapping into a set of cultural resources that recentre the role of elders "who had been marginalised through various colonial practices" but who actually have retained traditional practices, native languages and "knowledges pertaining to the land, the spiritual belief systems and the customary lore of the community" (p. 111). I therefore realised that involving the elders in programming and content production as the political and spiritual authorities of the community is a decolonial critique of our society for neglecting their experience and, at the same time, a proposed alternative and counterhegemonic practice of appealing to them as wise guides. This also operates as a practice of activism internally, because it lubricates and consolidates the relational dynamics within the community, supporting the ethnic identity self-ascription of young people.

Valuing the Everyday While Deconstructing Stereotypes

What I have reported so far shows how Indigenous media immerse their audiences directly in the daily dynamics and relational patterns of Indigenous communities. It is precisely in this specific practice of self-representation that media practitioners perceive themselves to be decolonising the most. According to a Guaraní spokesperson from FM Quarahy, Indigenous broadcasters "decolonise" precisely because they care about the "day-to-day stuff" and are interested "in something simple." She maintained that everyday reality is assumed to be of interest to others because these others are immersed in it, not apart from it. This idea is also reflected in what a representative of FM Qadhuoqte told me: unlike those who manage the mass media, the Qom communicators "think about the simplest things," about "the good quality of life of communities" who only want to "live in peace and well." At first, I could not see the connection between little, ordinary things and decoloniality, but later, as I got to know more Indigenous media practitioners and talked to them, I understood. Ramos-Rodríguez's (2020) proposal to think of Indigenous radio stations as 'the phone of the poor' seems to head in this direction. His simile appreciates the community service role media assume, especially in isolated areas or those with limited access to information; it also highlights the socio-economic and infrastructural inequalities Indigenous radio production tries to address. However, I believe that what the Guaraní and Qom spokespeople wanted to express by associating media content production with the simplicity of the everyday life of communities goes beyond this interpretation. It rather implied alternative priorities to those dominant in media-making and its products. Media production is carried out according to a mutual and circular relationship between broadcasters and communities as a counter-hegemonic gesture challenging Western/Northern patterns of social relationships and cultural processes. Media products encapsulate the situated and embodied experiences of Indigenous peoples, injecting their own dynamics and relational practices (that would otherwise be invisible) into the media supply as an alternative relatedness. In this regard, Almendra's (2010) idea of communication as a textile seems apposite; it immediately brings us into the (inter)weaving of relationships and activities that invigorate Indigenous cosmovision and ancestry. And just as how in the Nasa communities in Colombia communication springs from the sound of the river or the song of a bird, so on Qom radio FM Lqataxac Nam Qompi, for instance, the sound of nature pervades the morning programmes, when broadcasters play on "the sound of the sunrise birds: as the neighbours have a lot of chickens, here they are the roosters knocking at the door" to wake listeners. Likewise, Qom radio FM Viquen often plays a genre of music that "makes you think . . . of when you walk in the mountains and hear the songs of the birds or the noise of the river." Mapuche radio FM Nahuel Payun uses, as "the phonetic of the radio" (when it is active), the sound of the *Kultrun*, "a sacred element used by the Mapuche woman, . . . which represents the land"; this instrument is also the intended logo of the radio because "it is the radar that emits our sound, our voice and our thought." What makes Indigenous media recognisable is this familiarity and sensitivity of communication that reproduces Indigenous cosmogony.

These 'embedded aesthetics' (Ginsburg, 1991, 1994) allowed me, like any other listener, to grasp the spirituality that imbues the Indigenous understanding of communication and vitalises their community dynamics. This is what turns the media into 'alternative forms of cultural mediation' (Salazar, 2002) of such understanding and dynamics. They put their proposals into practice; they give an example-in-practice (the 'media-in-practices' defined by Mattoni, 2020) of how to put places and relationships at the core of social dynamics. In making such cultural objects (e.g., a radio programme about Indigenous music or cooking), Indigenous media-makers actually forge cultural processes (e.g., rooting music or cuisine in everyday practices) and thereby reproduce what the Guaraní leader of FM Ñandereco labels "the essence," that is, Indigenous cosmogonies anchored in identity, territoriality, languages, spirituality, autonomy and sovereignty. This is where I understood what the 'poetics' (Salazar & Córdova, 2008) of Indigenous media are all about and how they become an effective strategy for the generation of counter-discourses and alternative public spheres. The rescue of communal lifeforms and everyday dynamics ends up being a resistant and propositional alternative to the dominant social order.

Indeed, a Diaguita Calchaquí member of FM Mukarra, who also spoke about the radio as a means to transmit "the feelings, the essence" of the Indigenous context, added that such an essence is what makes one realise "the difference in how things are done or said" in Indigenous communities. It has to do with what she called "a feeling that makes [Indigenous people] fight and stay" in the face of a dominant culture. Embedding and broadcasting Indigenous spirituality in the media is a counter-hegemonic gesture, a demonstration of the political agency of Indigenous peoples inherent in the cultural creativity of their media practices (Himpele, 2008). By directly expressing their communities' reality, Indigenous media restore the value of places, history and lived experiences (Cerbino, 2018). They dignify the "traditional senses of social relatedness and communal orientations" in opposition to the inadequate "construct of 'community' as understood in contemporary terms" (Nakata, 2013: 130). At the same time, mediated communication contributes to "shap[ing] people's sense of identity, their sense of belonging and agency, and togetherness" (Rodríguez et al., 2014: 160), thus supporting the ethnic self-ascription of Indigenous peoples. All of this was precipitated in the 'Communication with Identity' proposal, presented by Indigenous organisations in Argentina during the public debate on the LSCA, which involved both the (re)construction of notions and meanings about what being Indigenous means and the disruption of imposed ones (Harris, Carlson, & Poata-Smith, 2013).

Following this reasoning, Indigenous peoples take back control of their own public image (Córdova, 2011) and affirm what Ginsburg (2016) defines as 'media sovereignty' (to extend the coverage of sovereignty "to the possession of technical, cultural, political and creative control over media produced by Indigenous peoples and about their lives," p. 583). This means self-representing Indigenous lifeforms and traditions in the media while challenging biased narratives about the Indigenous world. This is what, according to Castells-Talens (2016), makes Indigenous media a 'dissonance factor' altering official discourses about Indigenous peoples. This point is also clearly stated in the final declaration of the I Summit of Indigenous Communication of the Abya Yala (2010), when it urges public and private media "not to continue reproducing discriminatory practices of the image and culture of Indigenous peoples . . . that misinform, violate and devalue . . . native identities." I realised the actuality of this issue when the coordinator of FM

Nahuel Payun complained about commercial and government media "that are killing [Indigenous populations] little by little" by depicting them either as "good" or "annoying" depending on the patronising or criminalising attitude assumed. He observed that "when the Mapuche talk about their own loom [or] spinning, . . . or about the language [and] the dances, they are [perceived as] divine"; something that Castells-Talens (2016) would ascribe to their fulfilling the social expectations of white society regarding the *indio permitido*. Conversely, "when [the Mapuche] discuss territory, that's where it all ends," precisely for contravening to those expectations. "We are not folklore!" he added. Indigenous media fight this folkloric/criminalising game that underlies both the hegemonic media and the nation-state project.

The same interviewee highlighted that, in his experience, media practitioners aim to demonstrate that Indigenous peoples "are not [only] subjects of social rights, [but also] subjects of political and territorial rights; and [they] do not want political dialogue, [but rather] political debate." This statement indicates the extent to which Indigenous cultural vitality is intrinsically political, something evident in the cultural programming of the media outlets I visited. It was not just about reflecting ceremonies or beliefs in media content but of proposing different lifeforms and ways of staying in the world to the dominant by stressing the dimensions of spirituality, sociality and togetherness. Take local festivities, which according to Gutiérrez-Chong (2007: 315) "are one of the most advantageous settings for the realisation of ethnic projects": during *Pachamama* celebrations, the Carnival or the arrival of the New Year, Indigenous practitioners at many radio stations in the North-West play typical Andean dances or talk about "what is offered to Mother Earth, what giving her food, drinks, coca, cigars actually means." In transmitting and mirroring these festivities, media retrieve and sponsor them (cultural activism) while publicly legitimising their own beliefs and rituals (political gesture). Anyone listening to these programmes will have the impression that the Indigenous world, made up of allegedly obsolete rituals or beliefs, actually lives on today, suggesting alternative worldviews and practices. Something similar happens with traditional medicine. For instance, FM Whipala invite "professional nurses [to] talk about Indigenous health," while FM Ñandereco has "the programme 'Teko kabi,' which . . . is like a medley of many things [about] ancestral medicine." These programmes culturally enhance an equally effective holistic approach to health as a timely alternative to the dominant one.

Breaking Monolingualism Towards an Intercultural Dialogue

One of the decolonial efforts of Indigenous media practitioners that struck me the most concerns the recovery of native languages in media production and content. I realised the scope of this when a Comechingón Sanavirón spokesperson told me that the main challenge of their radio station is to "decolonise . . . the message, . . . the word." Many native languages have been lost because, for centuries, Indigenous peoples have been forced into not using them for fear of repression and discrimination. They functioned, in short, as a recognition device that activated discriminatory dynamics based on race. The languages, numbering over 1700, that existed during colonisation were first denied, then neglected and later folklorised (Gómez-Quintero, 2010). Various forms of linguistic disciplining have followed one another since the Conquest: firstly, the supremacy of writing over orality, as part of a supposedly civilising project aimed at universal literacy (Teuber, 1996); then, the choice of Spanish as the official language of the new nation-states, imposed by the *criollos* who led independence (Moreno-Fernández, 2006). The surviving languages were relegated to an underground resistance until the second half of the 20th century when cultural homologation driven by globalisation heightened the threat of their disappearance. After all, as explained by May (1998: 273), "the subsumption of all minority languages and cultures in a given nation-state territory" has always served as "the preserve of the dominant ethnic group" so that any difference "can be tolerated . . . at best, in the private domain, but any public recognition of . . . pluralism is ruled out of court." I heard of these mechanisms at work when the Mocoví representative of FM La Voz de los Pueblos reported to me that in schools teachers used to correct students using their native languages, while at home "elders stopped teaching the language to the children" so that, when they died, those languages died with them. These dynamics perfectly fitted in with the Argentinian nation-state building policies that sought to eradicate cultural differences within its borders. Even today, despite current policy efforts to include native languages in schools and media outlets, colonial languages prevail and make everyday inroads into Indigenous communities (Todd, 2013). This was clearly stated by the representative of FM Quarahy when he said that the Guaraní language "is running away" because "a lot of foreign language (i.e., English alongside Spanish) is coming in."

Veronelli (2015) calls this seamless process the 'coloniality of language,' that is, the racialisation of colonised populations as communicative agents; it has been deployed through monolingual ideology (that hides colonial oppression) and contempt towards native languages (interpreted as expressions of inferiority). Castells-Talens and colleagues (2009), on the other hand, speak about 'shy languages' when referring to native ones. I particularly value this expression because it captures perfectly both the shame and concealment imposed by coloniality and Indigenous efforts nowadays to recover, not without embarrassment, original vocabularies and grammars. I noticed this shyness, for instance, when some Guaraní and Kolla communicators told me that their radios broadcast in Spanish because not even the *Mburubicha* (the political authority of Guaraní communities) speaks the native language, or that the Quechua language is not an option for radio programmes because there are no listeners that would understand it. Currently in Argentina, only Qom and Mapuche broadcasters can adopt bilingual programming, since the Qomlaqtaq and the Mapudungun are the only native languages that have survived to any significant extent. For example, Wall Kintun TV edits and broadcasts documentaries that teach numbers and colours through Mapudungun cartoons, while FM Viquen broadcasts the news in Qomlaqtaq precisely to assert "the right to speak one's own language." In this regard, something particularly interesting was related to me by one of the Qom radio operators at FM Lqataxac Nam Qompi: she perceived that it was the microphone itself (a synecdoche for radio) that took the Qom people out of their shyness about speaking:

> The microphone is something that helps you a lot to strengthen linguistic competence: what always characterises the Qom people is that they are shy, they don't speak, they don't participate, and I think it's because of lack of practice. And you notice it a lot in those little ones (i.e., young people) who are already on the radio: they have no difficulty, they speak as if it were nothing.

All these testimonies demonstrate that, when it comes to languages, the first step on the path towards self-determination indicated by Tuhiwai-Smith (1999), namely, cultural survival, is particularly challenging but equally urgent for the majority of Indigenous peoples living in the Argentinian territory. The near disappearance of native languages is the most striking cultural legacy of the denial of otherness that has characterised the country's political history. As Cerbino (2018) states, media practices can reverse this legacy and help recover these languages as a political gesture in breaking the linguistic and semiotic domination created by the monolingualism of colonising cultures. Native languages are the sign of a way of life and a crucial component for augmenting self-determination. Speaking and listening to one's own language helps individuals and communities to recognise themselves as Indigenous; to network with other communities and strengthen the sense of belonging to an Indigenous nationality; and to gain public recognition from nation-state governments for Indigenous sovereignty based on cultural distinctiveness (Viatori & Ushigua, 2007).

The recovery of native languages through radio programmes or videos encapsulates both the defensive and propositional stances of Indigenous activism: the resistance to a history of invisibilisation perpetrated by the dominant culture and empowerment in asserting Indigenous identity and autonomy. Moreover, for Indigenous media practitioners, returning to the use of native languages reinforces ethnic identity self-ascription by insisting on the importance of recognising oneself in original linguistic codes. This is the reason why many broadcasters try to engage the few brothers or sisters who still speak native languages with educational programmes. FM Monte and FM El Antigal, for instance, invited some speakers of Quechua to teach it both to other radio staff and to listeners, while the FM Aim Mokoilek team is preparing a dictionary so that, by repeating words, listeners and speakers can memorise them. Furthermore, the Diaguita Calchaquí and Kolla radio stations are currently embarked on the cultural rescue of native languages by using some words that recur in everyday vocabularies, such as "the names of animals, plants, foods" (FM Identidad) or "some names of places" (FM Mukarra). As Ramos-Rodríguez (2020: 120) explains, this rescue of native languages gives them "vitality" and normalises them "in everyday environments" while inextricably linking culture and languages into "an indivisible duality" that "impacts the way one sees the world and builds identity."

Yet, even in cases where the native language is spoken fluently and is thus rooted in the daily use of communities, Castilian remains. The Qom and Mapuche radio practitioners continue with bilingual programmes instead of in purely native language ones, especially when it comes to denouncing what is happening in the territory. They retain the colonial language although they could renounce it (given their native languages are the only ones to survive); this constitutes a political re-signification of its use (Viatori & Ushigua, 2007). The communicators of FM Lqataxac Nam Qompi and FM Akukiche talk of bilingual programming "as a pedagogical tool" that educates non-Indigenous listeners on how and "why we are in this territory." Resorting to Castilian is, therefore, a voluntary media choice which underlies a political goal: it responds to the need to interact with wider audiences and broaden the scope of decolonial work through media content. This choice represents the endeavour to enter into dialogue with the non-Indigenous world.

This reasoning also explains why many broadcasters include non-Indigenous content in their programmes. FM Nahuel Payun, for instance, broadcasts a "sport programme . . . about basketball, football, boxing [alongside] the *palín*, a very typical sport of the Mapuche people," whereas FM Quarahy is famous for playing on and explaining the origins of *pin pin* or the *arzu tubasu* (Guaraní dances), along with typical dances of Argentine folklore. This syncretism between Indigenous and non-Indigenous content (Ginsburg, 2016) does not jeopardise the decolonisation objectives pursued by Indigenous broadcasters (Schiwy, 2009). Indeed, as the coordinators of FM El Antigal and FM Inti Puka explained to me, it "open[s] the radio stations up to the audience in order to capture it." In the experience of Indigenous media practitioners, when programmes are hybrid, they can be more attractive (especially to young people) and so reach wider and different audiences to whom Indigenous communicators can then also relate their own version of history and share their own traditions. Moreover, some media practitioners follow strict hybridisation logics to keep the programming faithful to the very concept of what Indigenous communication (including mediated communication) is and should be. To explain the Diaguita Calchaquí cross-pollination logic, a communicator from FM Itay Kaimen gave me the example of the *cumbia*, a popular Colombian song and dance which has spread through Latin America and become deeply rooted in Argentina:

> If you broadcast *cumbia*, you must respect the parameters that the community wants to endorse . . . We do not deny that *cumbia* has penetrated our territory, but we know that it is not our own music . . . We move the body because we have things to express, we have fun . . . but, in the end, there is a much deeper identity dealing with our people, our culture . . . Nowadays we dance *cumbia*, but two hundred years ago we danced to an ancestral music or . . . we sang our own music, which has much or even more value than [musical genres] coming from outside.

I understood in this the concrete meaning of what Harris and colleagues (2013) define as 'emergent' Indigenous identities, that is, identities that "are reflexively produced and depend as much upon the recognition of others as they do on the self-designations and self-attributions [they] assert during the course of social interaction with others" (p. 5). Dealing with coloniality implies acknowledging its existence and pervasiveness in everyday life (in this case represented by the *cumbia*), and from there trying to activate reflections that give both a greater historical depth to contemporary cultural practices (dancing per se) and an equal dignity to Indigenous ones (Indigenous dances). Colonial culture, then, activates sense-making processes that mingle conceptions and worldviews. In this sense, indigeneity is not about recovering purity or authenticity; rather, it is concerned with strengthening and maintaining an Indigenous identity while being immersed in the larger, dominant society. Indigenous peoples are engaged "in a constant process of endless and often unconscious negotiations between [Indigenous and Western] frames [. . .] for viewing, understanding, and knowing the world" (Nakata, 2007: 10). Western and Indigenous lifeforms interweave, compete and conflict every day, and Indigenous peoples traverse these intersections by "responding, interacting, taking positions, making decisions and in the process re-making cultures – ways of knowing, being and acting" (Nakata, 2002: 285–286). Besides, each people responds and remixes in its own way, which reflects the diversity of traditions and contexts, and the impact of colonisation (ibid.). Indeed, not all the Indigenous media practitioners I interviewed held the critical view of the Diaguita Calchaquí representative. For some radio announcers of the Lule

Vilela radio stations in Santiago del Estero, for example, Argentine folkloric music (e.g., *tango, chacarera, zamba*) is considered as their own traditional music. As already stated, they militate within the MOCASE-CV movement and thus draw upon the musical genres of the popular sectors (mainly peasantry) that participate in the movement. Thus, the boundaries between what music or dance is Lule Vilela and what is peasant must have been blurred in the meshes of a class struggle geared towards defending the land beyond ethnic affiliation. The trajectories of political militancy and the work of cultural recovery and development vary according to the places and histories of the different Indigenous peoples; this also makes a difference in how media content production is conceived and practised.

Being Indigenous is rather about becoming such within the negotiation of meanings that occurs when interacting with and contesting other cultural practices (Harris et al., 2013). Media provide the opportunity to observe and reflect on how to be(come) Indigenous. As a 'cultural interface' (Nakata, 2007), media allow us to appreciate the processes, constraints and opportunities at play in this be(com)ing Indigenous, backlighting all the contradictions and tensions of whether or not to align with Western agendas, objectives and working styles. In the hybridisation of genres and languages I saw a genuine operation of self-reflexivity alongside an open dialogue that welds decolonial critique and proposition together. This was very clear, for instance, in the vision of the members of FM Nahuel Payun. Their representative explained that "Indigenous peoples are fighting in all of Abya Yala [in order to have] a plurality of voices, . . . a single intercultural and plurinational society." In his view, their own radio

> surely must communicate with the identity . . . of the Mapuche people, but [also] with an intercultural perspective [so that] the radio can be interrelated [with that of other peoples'] and can also include the view of white people in its content; white people who are supportive of the Indigenous people's cause, . . . who think differently but sit down to debate the possibilities of this plurinational and pluricultural construction.

This demonstrates that, through "a more critical understanding of the underlying assumptions, motivations and values that inform [media] practices" (Tuhiwai-Smith, 1999: 20), Indigenous people raise awareness about a dominant culture that is transforming the Indigenous one so that, while decolonising the world outside, they must also decolonise themselves. As Rivera-Cusicanqui (2018: 122) states, "decolonisation begins at home"; in this case in the broadcasters' studios.

4 Management Challenges and the Media 'Battleground'

When I visited the Diaguita Calchaquí radio station FM Ambrosio Casimiro I was impressed by how concretely the territory and its embedded values entered the broadcaster. The building was oriented towards the West because, according to what the radio's managers told me, "the ancestors' pit houses were always built facing the West." They saw the radio's façade as a face, with two windows representing the eyes and the door the mouth. Each window had gratings in the shape of sacred Diaguita Calchaquí symbols: "the two-headed condor for air, the *suri* (a flightless bird found in the area) for water, the frog for earth, and the jaguar for fire." Traditional beliefs permeated the physical building, which was even anthropomorphised as an additional member of the community. FM Ambrosio Casimiro was there, towering over the communities, radiating Diaguita Calchaquí culture and conversing with the land. This made me realise that decolonial re-existence (Albán, 2013; Walsh, 2018) starts from inside, from transforming infrastructures and the logics of modern communication technologies through Indigenous sense-making and arrangements. As highlighted by Rodríguez and El Gazi (2007: 463), Indigenous peoples use multiple strategies in making media "tell the world in their own terms": not only by hybridising and mixing genres, as seen in the previous chapters, but also by "re-signifying established codes and conventions" and "re-inventing media institutions, organisations and even buildings." The 'media indigenisation/indianisation' (Salazar, 2002; Schiwy, 2009) also involves physical spaces and internal dynamics.

As Magallanes-Blanco (forthcoming) explains, "technological tools are transformed into relational objects and are objects of resignification of the daily practices of the subjects involved" thanks to self-reflexivity processes that flow within and between Indigenous communities. While debating the preservation of their physical and cultural integrity, reconfiguring cosmogonies within the current socio-historical context and facilitating internal organisation and participation, Indigenous peoples also "recognise flaws, weaknesses and contradictions that need to be collectively overcome" (ibid.).

DOI: 10.4324/9781003243083-5

Media are *catalysts* for all these processes in that they provide Indigenous people with the opportunity to constantly redefine indigeneity based on the need to adapt to the everchanging dominant society and analyse their own identity self-ascription in the making (the 'becoming-Indigenous' proposed by Harris et al., 2013) as a decolonial work that invests the self. Media are also *reagents* in that every Indigenous people or community reacts to the encounter/clash with coloniality and hence interfaces with media in their own way (Nakata, 2007), depending on contexts and trajectories. After all, Briones (2005) demonstrates that coloniality penetrated each Argentinian province differently, depending on both the local histories of the relationship with the state and the local constructions of indigeneity. By extension, this also applies to the penetration of communication technologies understood as artefacts and processes of modern culture. Through a permanent negotiation with Western/Northern standards and logics, each people, even each community reacts differently. In this regard, I agree with Zamorano-Villarreal (2009) when she proposes moving a step further from Indigenous identity politics enacted in/by the media. This perspective often depicts practitioners "as self-conscious agents who, by appropriating media technologies, are able to construct their cultural identities" and dispute the symbols and meanings that represent it; however, this focus might overshadow "the internal and external power relations through which Indigenous media are constructed, negotiated, and transformed" (p. 5). Exploring how Indigenous practitioners actually run the media meant seeing the other side of the coin and the contradictions inherent in Indigenous politics of self-representation.

On the other hand, during the interviews I understood that the application of the LSCA was a litmus test of how coloniality acts out through bureaucracy and institutions. While the state promotes Indigenous access to the media arena on paper, apparatuses and procedures interfere with their emancipatory processes in reality. The legal definition of Indigenous broadcasters as 'non-state public,' for example, is supposed to equate Indigenous peoples with the state because of their pre-existence and autochthony, thereby recognising their decision-making and managerial autonomy. Yet, to obtain the authorisation to broadcast first and then to win the FOMECA, they must certificate what they will do and how they will do it in order to be assessed by the state and meet the criteria which Western/Northern society think an Indigenous medium should meet. Not to mention that recognising the public but non-state status of broadcasters and authorising them directly for broadcasting does not exempt them from having to compete for funds in the same way as private non-profit media. This diversity of disciplines between (direct) frequency allocation and (competitive) resource allocation is a clear contradiction that reveals a lack of political will to create the actual conditions for broadcasting on an equal footing with the state. All broadcasters attempt to survive within a media system that is still pivoted around the logics of commercial and governmental sectors, despite the reform imported by the LSCA. They cope with economic constraints daily, which in turn lead to organisational difficulties and technical problems. In this dynamic, seeking economic support inside and outside Indigenous communities is combined with the effort to access public funds whose requirements, however, have nothing to do with Indigenous forms of living and projecting. Thus, economic sustainability works as a fertile ground for understanding the relationship between grassroots Indigenous activism and what Cerbino and I (2018) called 'state activism,' that is, its duty to enable concretely silenced social sectors to broadcast. It meant seeing the potentialities and contradictions inherent in the Indigenous attempt to gain recognition (the right to communicate) under the regime of state legality (the LSCA).

This chapter is structured around these two fields of tensions/negotiations with colonial modernity: running a medium and supporting it economically. As a 'cultural interface' (Nakata, 2007), the media allowed me to see how Indigenous agency is framed within a "push-pull between Indigenous and not-Indigenous positions" and to recognise that this "tug-of-war" creates physical tensions (p. 12) informing and limiting Indigenous decolonial responses. Firstly, I account for the internal dynamics that structure the broadcasters and the levels of indigenisation of what Gumucio-Dagron (2005) would call 'institutional sustainability' of the media (organisation, management and daily programming). Secondly, I analyse relational dynamics by age and gender, problematising the dangerous mixture of social roles in Indigenous culture and the stereotypes relating to the use of communication technologies. This offers some useful insights into the 'social sustainability' of media before focusing on the challenges that undermine their 'economic sustainability' (ibid.). Investigating the coping strategies adopted by Indigenous media-makers to survive reveals a daily effort to reconcile militancy and subsistence, adherence to Indigenous communication projects and meeting the demands of state bureaucracy.

Imprinting Commonality, Seeking Technicalities

When I interviewed Indigenous practitioners about how they run the media, they tended to divide it into three levels: organisation as the initiation phase of the communication project; management as coordination of daily activities; and the operational phase of broadcasting. In narrating the first two levels, a strong sense of commonality emerged. I refer to the practice and ethics of being with one another as an ongoing process for building decolonial futures. According to Altamirano-Jiménez (2020), commonality is mobilised by Indigenous people as an everyday exercise of their sovereignty towards

Western/Northern domination. On the other hand, Manzanelli (2020) shows that it includes a continuous, internal promotion of a sense of belonging by strengthening affective and cognitive ties between members while raising their awareness of a common past (i.e., 'communalisation process'). Commonality, in both its inward and outward decolonial character, is usually performed in community assembly, the plural political space in which the community collectively debates disputes and projects, drawing upon ancestral knowledge and values. Members of the community come together, see each other face to face, and express their individual thoughts until flowing into a single communal voice that exceeds the sum of its singularities (ibid.). In my experience, their decisions and principles reverberated in the organisation and management of Indigenous media as an imprint that influences the editorial line and decision-making processes. The broadcasters became part of the textile, described by Almendra (2010), as actual nodes contributing to the political project of self-determination. At the same time, they activate a 'self-reflexivity' process inside the communities (Magallanes-Blanco, forthcoming) which, while steering communication projects, find themselves talking about territorial struggles, cultural promotion and shared values.

This anchoring between the assembly and the medium varies according to each people's decision-making processes, its networks and the trajectory of political activism. In the case of the Diaguita Calchaquí people, for example, the organisational phase of all radio stations in the province of Salta was particularly sophisticated. The communities, which are used to working together on every project they undertake, simultaneously started the paperwork for the authorisation to broadcast and shared the self-training sessions on communication with identity, capitalising on the reasoning shared during the discussion of the LSCA. The assembly of each community discussed the name of each radio station, the team in charge of it and what topics to address on it. Subsequently, it designated a delegate for each radio station responsible for managing and supervising operational tasks under a common framework defined with the delegates from the other communities. In this way, the Diaguita Calchaquí radio stations operate in unison, filtered by the harmonising management of the delegates, while gathering the specific needs of each community as imprinted by the assembly upstream. The Guarani community in Misiones found its link to the radio instead by inserting a member of the council of elders into the management team to represent the political authority of the community in its daily operational activities. The preservation and intergenerational handover of ancestral values are very important needs in the agenda of the community, which experiences significant dispersion of its younger members and inhabits a rural area of the province remote from other Indigenous communities. Placing an elderly representative of the council in a radio team mainly composed of young people would ensure a balance between the youth pushing the station's activities towards Western/Northern media logics and the elderly anchoring it to Indigenous ones, within an intergenerational exchange that would bring the former closer to their ancestral roots and make the latter more confident in the self-representation possibilities offered by modern technology. This attention to internal community cohesion was already noted by Wortham (2004, 2013) in her analysis of Indigenous video in Mexico, in which, however, the reflection of Indigenous dynamics within the media not only served to strengthen identity self-ascription within communities, but also to better defend it in the mediated public sphere. I saw something similar in FM Truwvliñ To Kom. According to its representative, "the community authorities thought all together about . . . what direction the radio should take," thus acting as a "filter" just like the other cases discussed so far. But this collective reflection, she added, was very lively because "the Mapuche people's decision-making process always works this way: we grab each other by the hair, but it is something that identifies us." She then anchored the ethnic identity of the radio to the 'communalisation process' (Manzanelli, 2020) that characterises Mapuche political activities. This made the radio solid enough inwardly to enter the media arena and outsource "the ideological load" (in her words, the task of saying "the things to fight for") to the media content supply, thus turning commonality into an outwards decolonial exercise (Altamirano-Jiménez, 2020).

Whatever formula is adopted, the principles driving community life are infused in the media, inspiring the internal management of daily activities (the second level) with co-responsibility and a sense of belonging to the whole communication project. This aspect strongly emerges, for example, in the testimonies of Kolla media practitioners in the Andean-influenced North-West. They aim to empower young people participating in radio activities by involving their parents in meetings or by calling for regular internal assemblies to schedule the programming collectively. As Schiwy (2003) also noticed in Andean video-making, solidarity-based team management is mostly inspired by the values of reciprocity and exchange. According to the coordinator of FM Pachakuti, "the responsibility does not fall all on one person, and the working groups feel a degree of responsibility." In these narrations I understood that the aim was to promote a sense of mutual responsibility both among individual participants and between them and the whole group, thus replicating at management level the commonality understood not as the sum of its parts but transcending them (Altamirano-Jiménez, 2020; Manzanelli, 2020). Doyle (2016) already noted this aspect in the two experiences of audio-visual and radio production she investigated. They refer to a specific Indigenous mode of 'bonding' that Soler (2017) also identified in Indigenous video in Chaco. Once the editorial line and the positioning of the medium is defined at the level of the community assembly, the management teams have autonomy for the programming;

however, a consensual collective dynamic is always sought as an expression of the horizontality of decisions and circularity of speech.

Nevertheless, this relationality model was not always inherent in the communication projects I came to know. In some interviews, the management team was described as centred on individuals (often the interviewees), on whose shoulders the burden and honour of managing the medium fell, either because of certain personal characteristics they possessed or due to a lack of interest in taking responsibility from others in the community. However, it is on the operational level of day-to-day broadcasting that I was able to best grasp such contradictions and see the tug-of-war between Western/Northern and Indigenous inputs at work (Nakata, 2007). Unlike what Cerbino (2018: 136) traces in many Indigenous radio stations in Ecuador, where the work of the communicator turns out to be "very different from the segmentation of occupations shown in commercial radios," in Argentina few radio stations have every member of staff capable of working indifferently as announcer, operator and clerk. The majority of the broadcasters specialise tasks, thus privileging efficiency over knowledge sharing. I was quite surprised by this choice but also realised that it might depend on a lack of critical training beforehand. Many teams seemed to have only assimilated the Western/ Northern conventions and logics taught during technical training, in contrast to what Wortham (2004, 2013) found among Indigenous video-makers in Mexico. Conversely, when training was done with a more critical attitude, the rotation of roles respected the Indigenous vision of knowledge sharing. The practitioners of FM Truwvliñ to Kom, for instance, were trained by some members of the CCAIA, who participated in the formulation of the 'Communication with Identity' proposal and then taught them how to approach even daily activities in a communal way, with skills and know-how circulating among all radio members. The case of Diaguita Calchaquí radio is particularly exemplary in this regard, since the communities even appropriated the moment of training, redefining it as an autonomous practice of sharing knowledge rooted in their own cosmovision. Every media practitioner knows how to do every task, according to the same conception. Conversely, in radio stations whose members were trained by professionals focused on technicalities, the opportunity to rethink the rotation of roles in terms of commonality was lost. The radio team at FM Ñandereco, for instance, went to Buenos Aires to learn and was told that "the ideal is to prepare and train each one for each function." Something similar occurred in Wall Kintun TV, where the coordinator "keeps the papers," one member "is dedicated to editing," another "does all the technical stuff," another "is the producer, reporter and host" and another "goes out to do the filming."

In this panorama of such diverse experiences, I realised the complexity of the negotiation between Western/Northern and Indigenous logics described by Salazar (2002, 2014). But above all, I understood the scope of Zamorano-Villarreal's (2009) proposal to problematise how coloniality influences the inner processes of media-making. I did not find the primacy of subject above technique nor even the distancing from formal media-making that research conducted in other Latin American countries accounts for (see Schiwy 2003; Córdova, 2011; Wortham, 2013; Cerbino, 2018, among others). I noticed instead a demand for expertise and competence that most of the time implied an underestimation of the unconventional ways of doing media. In this regard, what the coordinator of FM Comunidad told me was particularly indicative:

> It is with [the FOMECA technical training] that we were able to . . . learn and write a script, and . . . to *correct some mistakes* . . . At the beginning everything was mixed up . . . and there was no rule guiding us to respect a schedule for each programme . . . Later, when we managed to get training, we started to make *real programmes*.

He associates the appropriate form of producing media content with the application of mainstream technical rules; this renders the 'embedded aesthetics' (Ginsburg, 1991, 1994) and the 'poetics' (Salazar & Córdova, 2008) of Indigenous media "mistaken." The alleged chaotic nature of initial activities is conceived as wrong, to the extent that only subsequent mainstream technical training made the programmes "real." Thus, the richness of the different times, ways and logics of making news or entertainment which, during the I and II Continental Summit of Indigenous Communication of Abya Yala, several Indigenous communicators valued as a real possibility for expressing their cosmovision in the media (Doyle, 2015a), is not appreciated by the Guaraní practitioner. I saw in his outlook how coloniality might infiltrate not only the management and broadcasting techniques per se, but also the very notion of what constitutes a good media product. In this regard, some Indigenous media practitioners in Mexico (Collective Author, 2018) speak about a 'little coloniser' living inside Indigenous peoples, a descriptor I find effective in accounting for their unwitting mechanisms of self-censorship and their reproduction of mainstream media structures and dynamics.

Plodding Through Age and Gender Roles

This negotiation between Indigenous values and Western/Northern logics also affects the internal division of roles between older and younger generations as well as between men and women, thus highlighting how Indigenous and colonial relational models can intermingle in discriminatory ways. As Carrillo-Olano's (2016) experience also demonstrates, entering Indigenous media allows us to see how the domination logic might be reproduced in those relationships "in which the older ones are right over the younger ones or where the man is worth more than the woman" (p. 201). The distribution of tasks in the media I accessed follows criteria that combine age– and gender-based roles, specific to the communities' lifeforms, with ageist and sexist stereotypes that often appear in Western/Northern society when talking about media usages.

Regarding age, in the previous chapter I already emphasised the importance of cross-generational transmission of knowledge in Indigenous lifeforms and the role that radio plays in strengthening the ethnic affiliation of younger people internally while promoting a different understanding of the role of older people in society externally. Here though I want to stress how some ageist conceptions related to the use of communication technologies combine with these Indigenous inter-generational dynamics in stigmatising ways. In many stations the elders do not participate in broadcasting operations but are relegated either to the role of supervisors of communication projects or speakers in cultural programmes, in accordance with their function as wise leaders. Conversely, teenagers and 20-year-olds who become acquainted with communication technologies in school and university are considered as experts in their use, such that they are treated as the repository of technical know-how par excellence, and that alone. They are described as "much more adept at handling the radio" (FM Ñandereco, Guaraní) and "quicker to grab hold of technological staff" (FM Ruina de Tinti, Diaguita Calchaquí), whereas the elderly can just "tell you a lot of stories" but "hardly know how to edit [them] for the programme" (FM El Puerto, Huarpe).

All these narratives essentially polarise the media roles according to an ageist view of both the use of communication technologies and ancestral knowledge transmission. The young are perceived as competent in the former and can learn about the latter; older people, on the other hand, have much to teach about the latter and are incapable of learning about the former. Somehow, the transmission of knowledge is thought of as a one-way street (from the elderly to young people, and only regarding Indigenous traditions), with no provision for the reverse (young people teaching older people how to use technological equipment). In this way, the elderly internalise the stereotypes and avoid technical operations. From the interviews, they even seem to distrust technology, because such an internalisation of media-related stereotypes combines with the 'shyness' (Castells-Talens, 2016) of speaking the native language or promoting ancestral culture publicly, after many decades of discrimination and silencing. This is something I heard about when the representatives of FM El Puerto, for instance, told me that, in the start-up phase of the radio, "the elders were afraid to speak, they were ashamed." Gradually, as they were interviewed by the younger members and spoke about traditional customs, they became familiar with the radio and understood that "their word does count." Something similar happened at FM Potae Napocna Navogoh, where the elders "never saw a radio . . . and were afraid to listen to each other" speaking Qom. There, the radio coordinators reassured them by explaining that they could speak freely because they were in a safe place. Likewise, in FM Akukiche the elders of the community were afraid, but the *Lonko* (the leader of a Mapuche community), who was "a young (guess what), educated man with a professional background" did teach them "at least to understand what the computer is." In this attempt to galvanise older people about public speaking on the radio, I found a solid intergenerational pact and the recognition of the social value of older people which I had already seen in the cultural dispute played out in the media. However, I also detected some judgemental attitudes, which are quite typical when people express opinions about the use of communication technologies by cohorts of other ages (Comunello, Rosales, Mulargia, Ieracitano, Belotti, Fernández-Ardèvol, 2020) and which are, therefore, transported into Indigenous intergenerational dynamics by the technologies themselves. The elderly adopt a sort of moralising attitude towards the young when legitimising their knowledge as the most authentic; on the other hand, the young patronise the elderly when making media know-how a prerogative of their own.

With respect to inter-gender relations, I also noticed a discriminatory mix between Indigenous social roles and media-related ones, especially when it came to the distribution of radio programming. The role of women tended to be restricted to the household knowledge that seems to be traditionally ascribed to them. On FM Ñandereco, for example, there is a programme called 'Only for women' in which "a woman from the community tells everything about what the *cuña* (the woman in Guaraní) is used to doing in her daily life for the home." A cooking programme at FM Inti Puka, in which recipes with products from the native mountains are broadcast as a practice of territorial struggle rooted in cultural programming, is run by women while men go out into the field to cover the conflicts. This role distribution even parallels the story of how the FM Mukarra radio station was built: "it was everyone's job, with the men of the community doing the roofing, and the women (guess what) the cooking." These reports resonate in Smith's (2016) interviews with Indigenous female video-makers, who describe themselves as dedicated to the culinary and artisanal tasks in their communities and act accordingly in the films. Carrillo-Olano (2016), in her experience with Indigenous radio-makers, also reports that women continue to oversee household care and child-rearing, thus remaining on the margins of many decision-making processes.

Schiwy (2009) argues that this role of women somehow values continuities between gender and knowledge: in the Indigenous films she analysed, women were guardians of traditions to be rescued and strengthened. This perspective resonates in the words of Moira Millán, a Mapuche activist who has led the *Movimiento de Mujeres Originarias por el Buen Vivir* in Argentina since 2015. In a recent interview with Margarucci (2019: 167), she recounted that Mapuche grandmothers "used to . . . heal with plants, . . . weave looms and speak Mapudungun," which made them "very powerful." Coeval women are instead "guardians of the land" and "warriors who must protect the life there," as a response to the current "neutralisation of Indigenous resistance" which is forcing men to move away (ivi: 172). However, notwithstanding the cultural and political value of women's knowledge deposited in care activities, and without neglecting the role that coloniality plays in reconfiguring gender roles in the communities it penetrates, it seemed to me that Indigenous women have an important role in the domestic/family sphere alone precisely because of these cultural beliefs. They end up being appreciated only for their re-creative capacity, be it physical (reproduction) or spiritual (education), which designates them as mothers and teachers (Magallanes-Blanco, Solana, Atala Layún, & Parra Hinojosa, 2012). This is something that Weise and Álvarez (2018) also found in other Latin American countries, where Indigenous women suffer from a lack of legal knowledge, violence and obstructionism to their leadership within their own communities.

Recently, Magallanes-Blanco and Monteforte-Bazzarello (2019) found that media enable Indigenous communities in Oaxaca (Mexico) to discuss women's rights and the need to eradicate all forms of gender violence. There, audio-visual production is based on investigations, discussions and reflections that are capitalised on by the communities to support the fight against the patriarchy beyond the media (ibid.). But I failed to find such radical questioning among the Indigenous media teams I interviewed in Argentina, nor even among women. It rather seemed to me that the self-reflexivity which media might activate and host (Magallanes-Blanco, forthcoming) was not so developed when it comes to recognising the patriarchal culture of Indigenous communities. For instance, the teams of the Lule Vilela radio stations boasted that they had decided to exclude offensive music content towards women; but this seemed to me the least they could do, even more so in a political context such as the one initiated by the Argentinian #NiUnaMenos movement which since 2015 has catapulted gender violence to the top of the national public debate. Nor do I think it is sufficient to dwell on the reasoning proposed by Ramos-Rodriguez (2016), by which the female presence in Indigenous media triggers a process of public visibility of women's problems previously relegated to the private sphere; if true, it is not enough. Re-proposing stereotyped roles of women and the underlying gender scripts in programming assignment further legitimises and reinforces them within community relations, in the mistaken name of tradition. I agree with Carrillo-Olano (2016: 205) when she argues that often "under the name of culture, [gender-based] relations of domination are taken for granted."

Yet, I must also admit that when I spoke with the Diaguita Calchaquí spokeswoman at FM Raíces, I had the feeling that some transformation was going on. She talked to me about the radio programme 'Things are ours' that she ran with two other women. It was "about different women's issues" and, according to her, it was "needed because the role of women is not like before: as far as cooking is concerned, now women occupy another space." This made me realise that at least half of the Indigenous spokespeople I interviewed were women, chosen as coordinators for communication projects. This means they hold a leadership role in the medium and that certain tasks were no longer the prerogative of men in many communities. This is something that, for example, Magallanes-Blanco and other colleagues (2012) found among Mixe women, whose self-esteem, sense of community belonging and political relevance had increased thanks to their involvement in audio-visual production. In Smith's (2016) interviews as well, some Indigenous women did hint at a change in gender-based social hierarchies within communities. Moreover, I realised that in many testimonies women were described as being engaged in operational broadcasting activities and as perfectly capable of handling audio-visual electronic devices. They were not portrayed as technically incompetent in the way I would have expected; they were rather legitimising themselves precisely through their technological skills. As Carrillo-Olano (2016: 205) argues, "women's participation [in the media] has become a strength for . . . breaking the myth that 'the technical stuff' is a man's area" and "demanding recognition and dignified treatment." According to the author, "it would be a lie to say that from the media . . . an equitable relationship between genders has been achieved" but media are working as "spaces where women fulfil [some] roles that break with historical structures of male domination over women" (ibid.).

As a 'cultural interface' (Nakata, 2007), broadcasters host the encounter between gender scripts of Indigenous tradition and Western/Northern sexist stereotypes, which end up being reinforced in the distribution of programming but also being challenged in operational roles, as a re-signification of established codes and conventions (Rodríguez & El Gazi, 2007). By the time this book is completed, things will have advanced. Several years have passed since the launch of both the #NiUnaMenos and the *Movimiento de Mujeres Originarias por el Buen Vivir*, so that the empowerment of Indigenous women (within and beyond the media) will have made great strides, also capitalising on the opportunity that media provide in questioning intergender hierarchies. According to Moira Millán, in Argentina, Indigenous women are leading a "process of change" as "producers of new theorisations . . . from [their own] ancestral ideology" (Margarucci, 2019: 172). She insists that they are fighting not as feminists but rather as anti-patriarchal, in that "patriarchy is a symptom of the colonising illness" (ibid.). Relmu Ñamku, another well-known female Mapuche activist, agreed with this position and stated that this is why Indigenous women "are pushing to incorporate [their own] particular situation [in the] feminists' political agenda"

(Wahnish, 2019: 161). This discomfort and difference with white forms of feminism also appears in the narratives of Indigenous women elsewhere (Magallanes-Blanco & Monteforte-Bazzarello, 2019), thus locating their political reasoning around gender at the crossroads between the recovery and development of ancestral culture and the complex alliances with other women's movements. It prefigures an intersectional dispute that re-defines coloniality beyond racial hierarchy; the media will have to be up to the challenge.

Juggling Grassroots Militancy and State Control

When delving into the meshwork of media management, some particularly challenging issues for Indigenous media practitioners come to the fore. Broadcasters live off the voluntary work of their few members and suffer an ongoing process of emigration of the younger ones. Fluctuation in member participation generates problems in the team's ability to plan programming and broadcast all-day long, every day. Besides, many communities lack the technical equipment or a studio and hence cannot go on air even if authorised. When they are active, they need to routinely update equipment and, in the process, sometimes accumulate debts for other expenses, such as electricity (expensive as the equipment consumes a lot of energy) and studio rent. Internet connectivity is lacking in many localities where the stations are based, therefore jeopardising news seeking and networking activities. And as if that were not enough, local atmospheric phenomena sometimes damage the equipment, while the mountains and countryside jeopardise the quality of transmission. This list of problems gives an idea of how the lack of economic resources, as a 'mother-problem,' has repercussions for broadcasting management.

Firstly, having no money hinders the remuneration and retention of media-makers. According to the coordinator of FM Quarahy, this is "the never-ending story that many media suffer . . . you start with the radio station, you go on for two or three months and then the young people . . . feel that they are losing time for not getting anything in return." This issue featured prominently in most of the interviews, suggesting that media activism is assumed by Indigenous media practitioners to be a militant commitment meriting reward. In this regard, I particularly appreciated what the spokeswoman of FM Ñandereco told me: "it would be nice to guarantee a salary for those who are dedicated to communication . . . which is what also the other journalists have . . . because if not, what are radio-makers going to live on?" In her words, Indigenous media-makers are equated to other journalists and for that they should be paid. It would be an economic incentive aimed at both sustaining their political motivation as activists and recognising their professional contribution as communicators. In a few interviews, however, an opposite view of media activism emerged, alluding to volunteerism as a yardstick for assessing the authenticity of members' commitment. As the spokeswoman of FM El Puerto stated, the lack of salary "is not a problem" because making radio "is not a matter of remuneration, [but rather] of militancy, regardless of whether there is [money] or not for those who are working in the radio." The underlying reasoning is that, since media-making is part of Indigenous militancy (in the very sense of 'media-in-practices' proposed by Mattoni, 2020), it absorbs its two main alleged features: not-for-profit motive and absence of professionalism. But this reasoning underlies both a confusion between profit and income and a biased distinction between grassroots and institutional politics. I understood this point when I spoke with the team of FM Inti Puka. They told me that "those who are in radio *like to feel* that they are working with new technologies, they *like to think of* themselves as journalists." Media activists are, therefore, described as 'fake' media practitioners due to a misconception of professionalism as something relegated to mainstream media and its techniques. However, this is a minority view among the teams I interviewed. The predominant opinion is that self-income should be provided to socially legitimise media-makers' contributions and recognise the media as self-managed social enterprises for cultural production.

Secondly, the lack of economic resources makes it impossible to bear the media maintenance costs. Teams are forced to invent and combine different fundraising strategies to meet the most urgent expenses, not without ramifications for the authenticity of the communication project. Sometimes they draw from community funds, consistent with the idea that broadcasters are part of the communities, which consequently have a responsibility to help them. In this regard, the spokeswoman of FM Maimará said: "since the beginning, the radio was thought of as purely communal, so it had to be supported by the fund that the community manages, the same as we do with the [other] physical spaces of the community." As the radio station is conceived as part of the community, all its members contribute directly or indirectly, even if they are not involved at a managerial level. This, in turn, entails a responsibility for each radio station as well. As the coordinator of FM Ocan highlighted, "the radio has to be an effective service for the communities, . . . so that people have, could or would like to contribute [financially]." This system, based on solidarity and mutual ownership, is consistent but not sufficient to move forward. Accordingly, media teams also organise social and cultural activities designed to raise funds quickly when faced with particularly large expenses. At the beginning, some of them organised *peñas* (popular musical parties) and raffles to buy basic equipment and launch the radio stations. Others routinely hold raffles and bingos or sell local products as systematic revenue streams to pay for bills and equipment maintenance. These types of initiative are sometimes accompanied by local-based advertising that, as Gumucio-Dagron (2005) has already pointed out, just serve to complement the array of self-managed options available to media teams without undermining the political and cultural project. For example, FM Whipala charges "local lamb [and] goat producers" for advertising, while FM El Puerto does the same with "Doña Rosa's kiosk next door," as part of a mutual benefit relationship between media and territory. Radio stations are important reference points for the local population and can therefore leverage this position to make some income; at the same time, they are part of that social fabric and, therefore, keep their advertising prices low to provide an affordable service to the community. This mechanism gets more complicated when the teams choose to advertise commercial businesses, since they must negotiate between opposing interests. For instance, the members of FM Inti Puka plan to advertise tourist enterprises in the area once they are on air and are aware that they must choose companies that do not damage the territory. The balancing act between the communication project's objectives and their guests' interests becomes even more complicated when the teams sell programming space to religious or political figures; sometimes it is the last resort, given the context. FM Comunidad, for example, is settled in a small community inhabited by a few families living off agriculture: there is no local business to advertise, so the radio team must sell some programming spaces to local politicians to maintain a minimum of income.

In this mix of self-managed strategies, a sort of 'joint and several liability' of community members coexists with more pragmatic logics. Interdependence and commonality as Indigenous values are reflected in the level of financial support, along with local-based advertising services provided by broadcasters in a quid pro quo based on solidarity. However, some fundraising choices are also driven by the mere need to survive with less attention to the risk of derailing the communication project. In this regard, the Mapuche spokesman for FM Nahuel Payun was particularly blunt:

> Our brothers and sisters must go around selling *chipa* (small cheese balls made from maize flour) or . . . firewood to manage to sustain their livelihood. So, we are going to revolt, and . . . to charge for advertising like any other radio station; and obviously we are going to all the politicians on duty asking for subsidies.

In these words, I identified a burst of anger and indignation that made me realise how staying in the media arena is a battle that Indigenous peoples want to win by any means necessary in order to dignify their 're-existence' (Albán, 2013). This is why all the broadcasters I reached also (try to) resort to public funding. As some Indigenous media practitioners in Mexico (Collective Author, 2018) stated, although interfacing with the state to gain public funds is exhausting, it is also a critical stance to affirm that public resources belong to Indigenous peoples as well. This strategy of economic sustenance, however, is a double-edged sword. On the one hand, it enhances the claim for the reparation of the historical debt that the state owes to Indigenous peoples; all the more so in Argentina that has tried to erase their existence from collective historical memory (Trinchero, 2009; Delrio, 2010). As a member of FM El Puerto told me, "if there is a law establishing that there can be Indigenous peoples in the middle of nowhere broadcasting, there has to be a state supporting them." While self-fundraising strategies informed by solidarity oversee the internal activism of Indigenous media practitioners, thereby contributing to the 'communalisation process' (Manzanelli, 2020), such a claim to the state feeds the Indigenous peoples' outward activism. As Cerbino and Belotti (2018) explained, it is a dispute over access to resources for the concrete exercise of those rights that would be otherwise recognised only on paper. On the other hand, the public funding strategy strengthens the economic dependence of Indigenous peoples on the state. They end up trapped in bureaucratic procedures and requirements, which work as controlling devices over their media power. And the application phase of the LSCA clearly demonstrated this. It was an ontic clash, which in turn underlies what Soler (2017) calls 'a clash of worldviews' between the state's inflexible and inhuman stance and the more fluid and flexible Indigenous lifestyle.

Indeed, all the Indigenous media practitioners met many obstacles to first obtain the authorisation to broadcast and then to win the FOMECA funds. They got lost in the bureaucratic requirements that oversee both processes since these impose forms of organisation that are very remote from Indigenous ways of life. The case of Diaguita Calchaquí radio is emblematic. The delegates had to "atomise" (as a representative of FM Ambrosio Casimiro put it) their radio experiences (belonging to the entire Diaguita Calchaquí people) and follow the law's logic based on single communities. Moreover, the Indigenous decision-making processes are ruled by horizontality and circularity, with long collective reflection and discussion. When combined with the lengthy bureaucracy and geographical difficulties of a federal state that centralises its administrative affairs in the capital city, communities get bogged down and take years to apply for and obtain any document. Drafting the required technical and cultural project, along with both a sustainability and a programming plan, is even more time consuming and requires Western/Northern knowledge of project writing which does not necessarily match Indigenous ways of thinking and planning. As the representative of FM Truwvliñ to Kom explained, "that's the part where you have to amass something new and good"; hence it takes time. In this specific request from the state, the coordinator of FM Pachakuti even saw a statement of superiority, typical of colonial domination: according to him, it was like "having to prove to the state that [they] were capable of sustaining and managing a radio station."

When it comes to competing for FOMECA, the process becomes even more difficult. Many broadcasters obtained their initial equipment by winning it in the 'Communication with identity' line of funding, which limited eligibility to authorised Indigenous communities. Most respondents assessed the FOMECA positively and appreciated the limiting of concurrency to Indigenous media. However, all of them complained about mechanisms and requirements, pointing to a lack of political will to support Indigenous broadcasters. The very choice of the competition mechanism is indicative of this. They had to fill out forms about the communication project, present three original budgets for the required technologies, detail the intended use of the money and justify the counterpart, that is, the part of the costs to be borne by the radio station itself. It is a lot of paperwork to be fulfilled by deadlines that are not even close to the Indigenous communities' timescales. The bureaucratic language is ambiguous, and getting the three budgets might prove impossible were there not enough businesses in the area. This is why many communities end up dropping out in the early stages of the process. Even setting up a bank account is complicated. As the representative of FM Pachakuti explained to me, banks require many documents as the basis for granting an account. Moreover, as FM team member Ambrosio Casimiro argued, maintaining it is too expensive for the communities. And once the funds are paid out, Indigenous media practitioners must account for their use, which is not always possible. FM Whipala, for example, used a local electrician to assemble the equipment, and he did not invoice them; likewise, the construction of the studio was done by community members, and these were not billable hours. So many communities end up winning the funds and not being able to use them. Finally, the obligatory counterpart absorbs the salaries of the media-makers most of the time; the banks retain a percentage of the funds and inflation (which is always high in Argentina) generates a significant price difference between estimated and actual costs.

This variety of situations paints a picture in which bureaucratic devices limit community access to necessary resources while disconnecting policies from the social actors for which they are intended. In this regard, the coordinator of FM Nahuel Payun denounced both the divide between the communities and the state apparatus and "the lack of commitment of many public officials" (who "don't go to the territory"). According to him, these two issues generate "a gap" that ends up functioning as a control mechanism of the state because the communities can only cross it "to the extent that [the institutions] allow it." Even when officials do go out into the field and commit themselves to a broadcaster, there is no guarantee that things could work out differently. As the representative of FM Itay Kaimen reported, officials end up "co-opting [the media] for political and personal interests," which is something that Indigenous media practitioners elsewhere also recognised, highlighting how "the co-optation of . . . struggles, processes and people, as well as . . . seeking economic resources from governments" lead to questioning the actual freedom of Indigenous media (Collective Author, 2018). This point was made very evident when I went to Wall Kintun TV and heard about its genesis. The project was originally set up by members of the 21-point Coalition. Representatives of a pro-Kirchner party managed it while young supporters of the Mapuche people oversaw the broadcasting activities. After several ideological clashes between the two groups, the latter left the channel due to suspicion of the former, who seemed to use it as a party medium. Therefore, new young Mapuche people were called for training by the party representatives, under the promise of a scholarship. However, this was never paid and they were even exhibited at official events with folklorising discourses that damaged the channel's image with Mapuche communities. To cap it all, when government funding was cut off, the institutional representatives left the channel, taking all the technological equipment. The current team took the trouble to reactivate it. They denounced all the events both publicly, before the *Defensoría del Público*, and in every Mapuche community in the area in order to regain their trust and restore the ethnic identity of the project. It was a difficult process, which accounts for how slippery the relationship with the state can become if communities and teams do not work together to delimit the margins of negotiation with politicians. As the experiences reported by Magallanes-Blanco and Monteforte-Bazzarello (2019) also confirm, any official dynamic of engagement with the government can generate influence peddling and political favours that end up damaging the real possibilities of an intercultural dialogue.

Conclusions

This book represents a journey through various Indigenous communities in Argentina, a journey on which readers have joined with me in visiting those broadcasters who act as touchpoints between Indigenous and Western/Northern societies. Media have worked as a 'cultural interface' (Nakata, 2007) which has allowed us to learn from the experiences of Indigenous media practitioners about the struggle of their communities and how they live. They have been "the point of entry for investigation . . . to explore the actualities of the everyday" (ivi: 12) and to recognise how the aspirations and lifeforms of Indigenous people compete, intersect and grapple with coloniality, understood as the never-ending process of physical and cultural domination of the West/ North. In Latin America, this process began with European colonisation, was formalised with the establishment of modern nation-states and subsequently consolidated with the arrival of global capitalism. In Argentina specifically, it consisted of a physical and symbolic annihilation of Indigenous peoples.

In this book we have seen coloniality at work on three specific battlefields related to Indigenous broadcasting media in Argentina: territory, culture and media management. In each of these fields we have observed the efforts of Indigenous media practitioners to resist on both physical/factual and symbolic/value levels as 'media-in-practices' (Mattoni, 2020) inherent in Indigenous activism for self-determination. The book goes beyond looking through a critical-analytical lens at media practices as political usages of communication technology; rather, it connects them to a broader and more painstaking work of decoloniality (Walsh, 2018). Hearing about how and why Indigenous peoples use the media was the gateway to understanding the political and cultural nature of their activism (what I called the 'matrix' of Indigenous media activism), what they contest, the alternatives they propose (the 'attitude'), and the effort necessitated both within the communities and towards Western/Northern society (the 'direction').

In these conclusions, I summarise and reflect on the main grassroots practices of Indigenous media practitioners on each battlefield (territory, culture

DOI: 10.4324/9781003243083-6

and media management) gathering them by matrix, direction and attitude. For each of these defining axes, I discuss the main strengths of Indigenous media activism but also offer critical insights where media practitioners can still improve in supporting self-determination in the current colonial scenario. Based on (the limits of) my research experience, I conclude with a brief reflection on what solidarity-based research can offer and the lessons to be learnt from Indigenous media practices.

The Political and Cultural Matrix of Indigenous Media Activism

The findings of the book show a dual political and cultural matrix in Indigenous media activism in that media practices, among other grassroots practices, encapsulate and interweave the political agency and cultural creativity of Indigenous peoples (Wortham, 2004; Himpele, 2008). With this juxtaposition, I refer to a collective counter-power exercised by Indigenous communities from the ground up, through and in the media as additional tools and spaces to dispute coloniality in its physical and symbolic expressions, and hence to affirm their ethnic identity based on cultural difference. This occurs, for instance, whenever Indigenous media practitioners use and conceive communication technologies as a constitutive part of protest/defence actions in and for territory. Broadcasting what happens in the ancestral territories and doing it from where it happens proved to widen participation in protest actions against extractivism and land usurpation, as well as being an effective protest in itself. Making news alongside protesters, based on the materiality of the persons and lands under attack, brings communities together (at least those belonging to the same Indigenous population) and interweaves their struggles (at least those carried on in the same region) while testifying to the Indigenous side of the story about coloniality from the experiences of those subject to it for centuries. Consolidating this networking capacity, therefore, allows Indigenous media operators to be more politically incisive and break out of the niche in which they still operate. They can create their own networks of Indigenous radio stations across the country, capitalising on those created during the LSCA discussion. These spaces give regular rhythm and national reach to the discussion on how to support local territorial disputes through radio activities, and how to keep the identity-cultural dispute in the concrete making of media. In addition, it is useful to participate in the community and alternative media networks already active in the country, such as the Argentinian Forum of Community Radio Broadcasters (FARCO) or the National Network of Alternative Media of Argentina (RNMA); even more so in the World Association of Community Radio Broadcasters – Latin America and the Caribbean (AMARC-ALC), which has hundreds of Indigenous and community radio stations affiliated in other Latin American countries. Although ontologically different from community and alternative media because of the ethnic identity shaping the communication project, Indigenous radio stations raise the same claims around why and how they stay in the mediated public space (Belotti, 2020). Joining forces is an effective political strategy to contest the dominant narratives about territorial conflicts underlying the hegemonic media.

Political, land-related defence also conveys the cultural promotion of Indigenous cosmogony inherent in the territory (Magallanes-Blanco, forthcoming); this works as an identity (self–)ascription device triggered by resistance to the material mechanisms of coloniality (e.g., land dispossessions, community evictions and environmental problems). Indigenous media help sustain the connection between humans and earth-beings through a different way of communicating which mirrors their own alternative way of inhabiting the world (Aguirre, 2002; Escobar, 2014; Magallanes-Blanco, 2015). They embed and transmit the holistic relationship with Mother Earth within media formats and contents without parcelling out natural resources from human communities, as is the case with the Western/Northern approach when extracting/exploiting resources and evicting communities (de la Cadena, 2015). Likewise, in recalling ancestral knowledge they keep alive their ancestors among the current inhabitants of the territories. In this regard, translating cultural baggage into images and sound (rather than just sound as the radio format does) might be more effective for communicating it to colonial society, especially outside Indigenous communities. When I met the reporter of Wall Kintun TV (long before interviewing him), I understood more clearly what constitutes dialogue with the *Pachamama* or the conversational scope of certain rituals. In his narratives about camera use during sacred celebrations or scenes broadcast in documentaries, I visualised more clearly the sacredness and knowledge inherent in nature. I, therefore, believe that Indigenous media practitioners should pressure state institutions more radically into creating and sustaining multiple Indigenous TV channels in Argentina. This also would allow them to access the transnational means of exchanging and circulating Indigenous videos, such as the Latin American Coordinating Committee of Indigenous Peoples' Film and Communication (CLACPI), which has proved politically and culturally empowering for media practitioners (Salazar & Córdova, 2008, 2019).

Culture itself turns into a politicised battlefield for affirming ethnic identity. Resistance to coloniality also takes place in the field of the symbolic, with Indigenous peoples revitalising beliefs, rituals and knowledge through/ in the media both for their own social cohesion and as political action against dominant cultures (Gutiérrez-Chong, 2007). Indigenous media break into the (mediated) public sphere to exercise their ethnic citizenship (de la Peña,

1995; Mata, 2006; Salazar, 2010) and as an act of recognition justice (Whyte, 2011, 2016; Salazar & Córdova, 2019) that conveys the historical continuity of Indigenous culture in response to the cultural homologation imposed by coloniality. By promoting orality through/in radio, Indigenous media-makers re-write official history with direct, collective testimony and bridge intergenerational gaps to oppose the de-indianisation of Argentinian historical memory. Through revitalising native languages, they break the discriminatory (self–) censorship mechanisms that have relegated Indigenous peoples to invisibility for centuries while opening a space for intercultural dialogue. When restoring the centrality of proximal relations and presenting Indigenous daily reality in media content production, they challenge the colonial social order with its criminalising and folklorising stereotypes about Indigenous peoples.

In the path towards self-determination, the struggle for ancestral territories and the dispute for Indigenous knowledge, traditions and beliefs imply each other; this is something that also resonates in recent debates on media cultures in Latin America, where the defence of life and territories (Magallanes-Blanco & Trerè, 2019) and the achievement of self-determination based on cultural difference (Salazar & Cordova, 2019) emerge as central axes of the Indigenous movements active in this region. This is why consolidating alliances and networks at a national level, as suggested earlier, would also allow the Indigenous media practitioners of Argentina to interface with and borrow practices from Indigenous and community radio networks active in other countries that count on a high Indigenous representation and activism, such as the Association of Radio Education (ERBOL) and the Radio Production Centres (CEPRA) in Bolivia, the National Assembly of Community Communication in Ecuador, or the Intercultural Communication Services (SERVINDI) and the Network of Indigenous Communicators (REDCIP) in Peru. These networks have years of militancy in the field of culture as a central area in striving for the self-determination of Indigenous peoples; they have made pluri-nationalism their strength in confronting colonial cultural domination. They could therefore effectively support Indigenous media practitioners active in Argentina in their political and cultural work.

As for media management, we saw the interplay between political agency and cultural creativity at work in the organisation of broadcasters, when Indigenous values give communication projects the stamp of Indigenous identity. Through various formulas, communal political assemblies act on broadcasters to make them both representative projects and integral parts of Indigenous communities. It is an osmotic exchange in which the principle of communality works as a device of both political sovereignty and internal cultural cohesion (Altamirano-Jiménez, 2020; Manzanelli, 2020). The communities' stance feeds into the editorial line of the media, while their values inform the criteria of media management, thus integrating political and cultural activism into the very design of communication projects. In efforts to sustain media activities economically, the cultural ability of Indigenous media practitioners to find self-financing mechanisms (which have the political value of reinforcing mutual ownership between communication projects and communities) co-exists with their political demand for the state to pay its historical debt to Indigenous peoples through public funding (which has a cultural repercussion by challenging Indigenous forms of living and planning). In this respect, consolidating the nationwide networks that emerged during the discussion of the LSCA, as mentioned earlier, can enable an exchange of experiences (about strategies for self-financing and public planning), which strengthen the skills of each media maker, thus making them even more culturally creative in self-subsistence, and politically stronger when knocking on the door of the state to claim the resources to which they are entitled. In many interviews, media practitioners expressed the need for technical support from the state to learn how to draw up the templates required for authorisation to broadcast or to design communication projects according to the logic of the FOMECA calls to tender. However, I believe that self-training in this area, capitalising on the experiences of those who have already learned or those who have found effective self-financing formulas, would make it possible to loosen the economic dependence that currently binds broadcasters to the state.

The Outward and Inward Direction of Indigenous Media Activism

The book has also made clear that the political and cultural activism performed by Indigenous media moves in two directions: outwards, when challenging and interacting with colonial society and its devices of physical and symbolic domination; inwards, when strengthening the political participation, social cohesion and cultural affiliation of Indigenous peoples. This is a simultaneous dual effort deployed by and in the Indigenous media, which contests and aspires to transform the West/North through Indigenous ways of living and communicating, while consolidating (self–)identity ascription within Indigenous communities and strengthening alliances between them (Schiwy, 2002; Wortham, 2004). The first effort supports the second in that the media make visible Indigenous reality by telling how they used to and still live, thereby enabling Indigenous individuals and communities to identify themselves with and embrace Indigenous struggles and lifeforms (i.e., the 'ethnogenesis' conceptualised by de la Peña, 1995 and applied to the media by Salazar, 2014). The second effort supports the first in that the media help to create a united front against colonial domination based on a solid sense of identity breaking into the mediated public sphere and, from this standpoint, raises issues about ethnic citizenship and recognition (i.e., the 'activist imaginary' conceptualised by Marcus, 2006 and applied to the Indigenous media by Ginsburg, 2011; Salazar, 2014).

This dual orientation is, for example, intrinsic to the territorial dispute. In denouncing what is happening in their own lands, Indigenous media practitioners rally support for the Indigenous cause from sectors of Argentinian society (outwards) and unite Indigenous communities scattered across the country (inwards). Defending Indigenous cosmogony inherent in the territory is both an invitation to Western/Northern society to rethink its relationship with the environment and natural resources (outwards) and the recovery/maintenance of original communicative and relational practices within communities (inwards). This dynamic between outside and inside is what allows for a stronger sense of ethnic identity and a more assertive confrontation with colonial power (González-Tanco, 2016). As spaces of ontological encounter/clash between two worldviews about territory (and every being that inhabits it), the media carry out a dialogue with both coloniality, through its languages and categories (mostly in the morning news bulletins, reporting what happens in the territories through the grammar of rights and grassroots militancy), and with the Indigenous communities, through their own knowledge and conceptualisations (mostly in cultural programming, by using native vocabularies and ancestral references).

This dual motion also runs through culture as a field of contention per se. There, media function as devices of re-existence (Albán, 2013) in that they revitalise traditions, languages and beliefs (internally), while dignifying them in the mediated public sphere (externally). Indigenous media serve to empower Indigenous individuals in their ethnic affiliation, while demonstrating to the colonial world that Indigenous peoples still exist. This latter issue is particularly cogent in Argentina which has historically proposed a '*sin indios*' nationhood (Trinchero, 2009). This is why, for instance, Indigenous media practitioners are committed to challenge official history with their own version in media programming, in schools, and in public commemorations of historical events. It is a situated exercise of collective memory that locates Indigenous cultural and political identity internally, whilst critiquing the oppression externally (Rivera-Cusicanqui, 2008). Through oral hi-storytelling, the recovery of native languages and intergenerational transfer, Indigenous media allows ethnic identities to survive and adapt over time within the colonial scenario.

In this two-way cultural endeavour, however, Indigenous media are also permeable. Practitioners are open to intercultural dialogue with the dominant culture and by hybridising music genres and through bilingual programming make room for it within Indigenous society. Moreover, they mostly embrace mainstream media standards when specialising in operational skills or adhering to strict programming scheduling, thus cross-pollinating typical Indigenous timeframes and ways of communicating with those of the West/North. This infiltration raises some issues. It is true that, outwardly, Indigenous peoples seek to assert themselves in the media arena with their own cultural and communicative processes based on communality (i.e., 'media decolonisation,' Salazar, 2010; Córdova, 2011; Cerbino, 2018). It is an exercise of "technical, cultural, political and creative control over media" (i.e., 'media sovereignty,' Ginsburg, 2016: 583) which aims at challenging Western/Northern media-making. It is also true that, inwardly, media teams work to consolidate and empower their own cultural and communicative processes (i.e., 'media indigenisation,' Salazar, 2002; Schiwy 2009; Doyle, 2015a) as social exchanges based on ethnic membership and its symbolic resources (i.e., 'ethno-communication,' Aguirre, 2002). Yet, both impulses crash both against the control devices of the state (e.g., templates and deadlines that do not match the decision-making of the communities) and the mainstream logics of media-making (e.g., those taught through professional training and uncritically assimilated by many media-makers). To cushion the first crash, it would be useful to open up negotiating possibilities with public institutions to rethink the procedures for access to radio frequency and funds, starting from the actual way in which Indigenous communities work. The outward-looking struggle is for public resources that concretely enable communities to produce media, and for public policies that are designed around their realities. In other words, it is a dispute for political recognition of Indigenous cultural capabilities proven by running their own media. To soften the second crash, it would be helpful to strengthen collective discussion (both within and between communities) to rethink media-making techniques and aesthetics, starting from the way communication is originally conceived and practised by Indigenous peoples. It would take a little more daring; the self-training of the Diaguita Calchaquí communities might be an exemplary experience in this respect. Moreover, intercultural associations and media could support this empowerment process in local settings. Experiences of this kind have produced effective results in terms of both inward and outward activism (Magallanes-Blanco & Monteforte-Bazzarello, 2019). In Chaco and Formosa, for instance, the Timbó news agency is already working in this direction with impressive results. Its members work closely with the Qom and Pilagá communities and train them in media-making by overcoming the mainstream mould and finding instead creative ways to translate Indigenous cultural practices into media content and management (Della Bruna & Slagter, 2019). Indeed, the inward-looking dispute is for the maintenance of ethnic identity throughout the media-making chain and for making the media consistent with the cultural processes and social dynamics of Indigenous communities (i.e., the 'poetics,' Salazar & Córdova, 2008). That is, it is a dispute about empowering Indigenous communities and strengthening their cultural identity as steps in the path towards self-determination.

The Destruens and Construens Attitude of Indigenous Media Activism

Finally, the analysis offered by the book revolves around the dual confrontational and propositional attitude of Indigenous media as decolonial activism (Walsh, 2018). Resistance and empowerment of Indigenous peoples materialise in media practices at the same time: they aim to dismantle physical and symbolic devices of colonial power while promoting cultural, political, social and economic alternatives from their own worldviews and habits.

For instance, while denouncing what happens in the territory, Indigenous media practitioners also propose another way of inhabiting the world and relating to nature. They alternate critical news-making (against the attack on and parcelling out of the territory that is typical of the Western/Northern conception, de la Cadena, 2015) and promotional cultural programming (in favour of the human ability to *sentipensar* with nature, typical of the Indigenous conception of territory, Escobar, 2014) in the attempt to provide thorough media content that holds together protest and prospect. Even in the most brutal content, such as the stories of Indigenous militants killed during police repression or at the hands of private assassins, these two perspectives co-exist. These situated, presential stories report events from the tragic experience lived by the *comuneros* as a response to the demystifying or criminalising narratives of the mainstream media (the *pars destruens*). At the same time, these stories express a desire to make known the ancestral principles and values for which they fight and to show why it is even worth dying to defend them (the *pars construens*). However, Indigenous cosmogony remains unclear to non-Indigenous audiences who prove supportive of Indigenous struggles but not necessarily aware of the different ontology found in ancestral territories. To strengthen the *pars construens*, therefore, Indigenous media practitioners could organise workshops and seminars open to non-Indigenous society (e.g., social organisations, community radio stations, alternative television channels) to find complementary forms to transmit their distinctive way of inhabiting the world.

The dual confrontational/propositional attitude is also constitutive of Indigenous media activism on the battlefield of culture. For example, the oral reconstruction of the genocides that first occurred during European colonisation and subsequently in military campaigns by means of radio history programmes or documentaries serves both to contest official history (which denies the existence of the Indigenous people as symbolic capital of the Argentinian nationhood, Briones, 2003) and promotes the vitality/validity of original forms of cultural production (supplanted by colonial written literacy, Teuber, 1996). Likewise, the centrality of intergenerational transmission of knowledge between elders and youngsters who 'meet' on the radio both questions Western/Northern forms of producing knowledge and marginalising the elderly, and emphasises their social utility and the topicality of their experience. Furthermore, the recovery of native vocabularies within bilingual programming incorporates both a critique of colonial monolingualism (Viatori & Ushigua, 2007; Veronelli, 2015; Cerbino, 2018) and the proposal to educate, with an actual pedagogical tool, non-Indigenous audiences about Indigenous reality. Knowledge circulation and cultural continuity both challenge the angular patterns of Western/Northern knowledge-building and fill the gaps left by such biased epistemologies (Santos, 2018) with new and more inclusive cultural practices. Again, it would be useful to transpose these to non-Indigenous spaces (e.g., alternative media, public schools and universities) to legitimise decoloniality as a practice of contestation and proposition beyond Indigenous circles and to infiltrate non-Indigenous society. The Timbó news agency mentioned earlier, which has made listening to diversity its main training tool, reports numerous successful encounters of this kind in Chaco and Formosa (Della Bruna & Slagter, 2019).

This dynamic of contestation/proposition also takes on relevance in media establishment and organisation. We have seen that Indigenous media challenge mainstream logics by customising the editorial line and the decision-making processes according to their own communal dynamics (e.g., co-responsibility, circulation of the word, and sense of belonging to the communication project), while proposing a different way of running media. Nevertheless, contradictory dynamics surfaced when investigating the operational phase of media management: dealing with alien communication devices and logics complicates the practical application of Indigenous dynamics in daily broadcasting activities. By running with the hare and hunting with the hounds, Indigenous media practitioners negotiate with media as modern devices and Indigenous principles as identification devices, thus leading to different outcomes in each broadcaster. For instance, technical and aesthetic protocols imposed by the colonial Western/Northern standards induce many Indigenous communicators to consider their own as mistaken and to imitate commercial formats. There is almost no critical attitude towards the specialisation of know-hows typical of Western/Northern enterprises, and, therefore, in most stations everyone has a specific role to play (technical operator, speaker, administrator). Only in a few cases is the Indigenous principle of knowledge circulation translated into role rotation and skill sharing. Therefore, it would be worth teaching praxeological media-making to future media practitioners, based on the application of Indigenous regulatory principles even in the operational phase.

Incorporating Indigenous protocols in concrete media-making (Ginsburg, 1991, 1994; Wortham, 2013) means legitimising them in the media arena, as both a challenge and a proposition. Moreover, I noticed in internal relations between different age groups and genders incomplete decolonial work. Indigenous media team members criticise Western/Northern society for trivialising and underestimating the wisdom of the elderly and the household knowledge of women. Hosting them in radio programming is a cultural proposal which alters modern ways of conceiving and approaching them. Equally interesting is the decolonial effort to anchor women's leadership precisely in their technological skills: these are always thought of as men's prerogative in Western/Northern society, with a lower emancipatory potential compared to what Indigenous women have shown so far. Nonetheless, the elderly are treated as being unfamiliar with technology just as in Western/Northern society, without criticism or anti-ageist proposals. Women are still relegated to domestic roles (both in media programming and in communities) within a still incipient depatriarchalisation of Indigenous culture. In other words, ageist conceptions of technology (characteristic of Western/Northern culture) and sexist conceptions of social roles (characteristic of both Indigenous and Western/Northern culture) distort programme allocation criteria and are barely questioned. Rather, Indigenous media practitioners should promote a broader reflection within communities on these phenomena at work in Indigenous society, using the media as an opportunity/space for self-reflexivity (Magallanes-Blanco, forthcoming). Experiences of this kind (Magallanes-Blanco & Monteforte-Bazzarello, 2019) have already proved effective. Tracing certain patterns back to the encounter/clash with the West/North (e.g., the ageist stereotypes attached to the usages of communication technologies) and others to Indigenous culture itself (e.g., the sexist social segregation of women) would help deconstruct them to build new inclusive forms of sociability.

On the terrain of economic sustainability, decolonial efforts undertaken by Indigenous media practitioners include both the prospect, in the creative forms of self-funding they find, and the protest, in demanding public funds based on legal rights. The former demonstrates that there are alternative and solidarity-based ways of financing media activities (and therefore of making communication) while respecting/strengthening the physical and symbolic link between communities and broadcasters. The latter has to do with demanding from the state what is historically owed to Indigenous peoples, and this is a tension worth maintaining permanently. In this, I agree with Gumucio-Dagron (2005) when he argues that "the ideal would be to achieve a balance between [. . .] the support of national institutions, [. . .] and the contributions of the community itself and of the media workers" (p. 16). Nonetheless, public funding might become a double-edged sword as long as there is a relationship of economic dependence disguised as a support. Consider the LSCA. Although on paper it places state and Indigenous media on an equal footing, thus recognising the autonomy of Indigenous communities from state interference (which is why most interviewees applauded the 'non-state public' legal descriptor of Indigenous media), in fact it limits this autonomy in the application phase, when it pegs the procedures of applying for broadcasting authorisation or for winning the FOMECA competition to the logic and requirements of the state (rather than the actuality of Indigenous ways of life). Bureaucracy becomes an instrument of control, and public funds function as a lure to maintain this control. A more radical dispute about the mechanisms that oversee access to public funds is necessary. Decolonial effort, therefore, could take the form of opening new negotiating possibilities where Indigenous media practitioners can give useful insights about how to streamline the procedures, advocate for Indigenous representation in the evaluation committee of FOMECA projects, or demand more effective mechanisms of direct funding. These points can be capitalised in specific forums for political consultation and discussion with public institutions (provided that these have an authentic political will to open up such deliberative spaces); otherwise, acquiring rights ends up just regimenting media practices within legality's affordances and constraints, thus limiting the political work pursued by Indigenous media practitioners. Besides, such forums would allow discussion of a further issue that encapsulates both a challenge and a proposal: the need to provide self-income mechanisms for Indigenous media practitioners. They deserve to be acknowledged as professional workers within the media industries (and beyond grassroots militancy) who can enrich media supply. Conditions must be created to make this possible within a modern colonial system that, instead, keeps relegating them to the margins and thereby sacrifices the cultural contribution they make to those industries.

Supportive Research in-Practice: Final Thoughts

In writing this book, I have come to identify a series of potential activities that researchers committed to accompanying Indigenous and other grassroots media from the standpoint of solidarity and service can undertake to expand and improve the conditions of media for social change (Tuhiwai-Smith, 2006; Krusz et al., 2020). For instance, they can pool their contacts gathered through (political, media and/or research) work in the field and act as a *trait d'union* between different Indigenous and community/alternative broadcasters, thus opening up a space for them to meet and discuss. They can moderate and narrow the discussion down to the critical points emerging in their analyses, while activists and practitioners look at their labour from a different angle and thus better understand its transformative scope and its possible limitations. This could favour a focused exchange of experiences that can help support territorial and cultural disputes through media activities. On the other hand, meetings of this kind can encourage the institutionalisation of a network, useful for supporting participation in regional networks of Indigenous communicators and getting identified at the international level. In Argentina, in particular, this exchange would also be beneficial for learning or inventing new self-financing strategies, while improving the projecting skills required by the state to first obtain radio frequencies, and then to compete for FOMECA. In this space, Indigenous and other media activists could also reflect on the self-income issue and its implications, coming up with some ideas on how to professionalise activist media-making in the media industries without losing either the activist character or Indigenous aesthetics and protocols. Likewise, a further and deeper discussion on how to deconstruct ageist and sexist stereotypes linked both to the social roles of the young/elderly and men/women and to the usages of communication technologies would be desirable; researchers' knowledge about similar experiences in other countries may help point out issues or practices that would otherwise go unnoticed.

This grassroots labour should be accompanied by a permanent dialogue with the institutions responsible for designing and implementing public policies on mediated communication, along with universities and research institutes. Committed researchers could push to open participatory workshops to discuss the current status quo and provide empirically based guidelines to change it by means of policy papers. In Argentina, for instance, they could bring together representatives from ENACOM, the *Defensoria del Público*, Indigenous media and networks of alternative media in order to rethink the procedures for broadcasting authorisation and funding, and increase the number of Indigenous television channels throughout the country. In such a space, researchers could play the role of mediators capable of raising useful demands to effectively democratise the media system and enhance the contribution of grassroots broadcasters. Universities and research institutes should also contribute to the opening of these spaces, with committed researchers pushing for a greater civic role and public engagement of these institutions through action-research programmes and cultural promotion in society that capitalise on knowledge for social intervention. All this, moreover, could have the advantage of having a retroactive effect on curricular teaching, enriching communication studies and social research with the militant and professional experience of Indigenous and popular media practitioners.

I choose to close this book with such a 'pragmatic' reflection about the research profession because I believe that committed, decolonising research is needed and should serve Indigenous communities in their political and cultural claims, in their inward and outward commitment to self-determination, and in deconstructing the colonial legacy while proposing alternatives that can be beneficial to society at large. I am thinking, for example, about the climate crisis we are experiencing nowadays and how much Indigenous cosmogony can teach us Westerners/Northerners about saving the future of the planet. It is no coincidence that as I write, the Zapatistas are travelling around Europe to meet different social movements active in the defence of ecosystems and biodiversity. There are still possible alliances to be forged, and those who do research must be able to facilitate these processes and enhance political action for social change. I am also thinking about gender violence that is reactivating an intersectional trans-feminist insurrection worldwide. This is challenging the hetero-patriarchal structure of societies; the self-reflexivity practices of Indigenous peoples can serve as an antechamber for drastic transformations. Researchers and activists, especially women, must feel called upon to take part in it, to translate knowledge into revolutionary practices.

Finally, I am thinking about the very meaning of communication and the timeframes and forms of media activism. We have seen that Indigenous media as cultural processes support the political dispute for autonomy and self-determination; at the same time, as political activities, they serve the cultural effort of (re–)defining indigeneity in the colonial scenario. Moreover, media practices are osmotically outward activities which support the upholding of 'being Indigenous' in colonial society, and inward processes which serve the effort of 'becoming Indigenous' within Indigenous society. Either way, communication is a claim for recognition of a cultural difference that is constantly defined within the relationship with coloniality. It is a critique of the colonial power and of what being Indigenous is not and never was; it is a proposition of different ways of living and hence of what being Indigenous actually means. Indigenous media teach us to recover the multiple dimensions of the meaning of communication itself that unfolds in technologies while transcending them. It is a weapon for defending the territory but also *sentipensar* with it; it is transmission of knowledge and historical reconstruction as a political strategy of survival and cultural performance of re-existence; it is the bundle of proximal relations on which all this rests; it is the opening to interculturality within a permanent rethinking of coloniality; it is the field where encountering/clashing with both the mechanisms of state control and the standardised/stereotypical usages of modern technologies. All this challenges studies on media (and) activism by inviting us not to focus too much on the uses of communication technologies but rather to understand the underlying disputes and power relations being communicated. It shows us the relevance of alternative living models and the determination of identity processes that would otherwise be trivialised and marginalised within the academy. It teaches us how to rethink research practices starting from the praxes of those who 'do the things' we study.

References

Aguirre, J. L. (2002). Bases para comprender la comunicación. *Punto Cero, 7*(4), 47–49.

Albán, A. A. (2013). Pedagogías de la re-existencia. Artistas indígenas y afrocolombianos. In C. Walsh (Ed.). *Pedagogías decoloniales: prácticas insurgentes de resistir,(re)existir y (re)vivir.* Vol. 1 (p. 443–468). Quito: Abya-Yala.

Almendra, V. (2010). *Encontrar la palabra perfecta: experiencia del Tejido de Comunicación del pueblo Nasa en Colombia.* Master's thesis, Universidad Autónoma de Occidente, Cali, Colombia.

Altamirano-Jiménez, I. (2020). Communality as everyday indigenous sovereignty in Oaxaca, Mexico. In B. Hokowhitu, A. Moreton-Robinson, L. Tuhiwai-Smith, C. Andersen, & S. Larkin (Eds.). *Routledge handbook of critical indigenous studies* (pp. 337–346). London: Routledge.

Amnesty International (2017). Relevamiento sobre los conflictos indígenas en Argentina. Retrieved November 2, 2021, from www.territorioindigena.com.ar/.

Arcila-Calderón, C., Barranquero, A., & González-Tanco, E. (2018). From media to Buen Vivir: Latin American approaches to indigenous communication. *Communication Theory, 28*(2), 180–201. https://doi.org/10.1093/ct/qty004

Atton, C. (2002). *Alternative media.* London: Sage.

Bakardjieva, M. (2015). Do clouds have politics? Collective actors in social media land. *Information, Communication & Society, 18*(8), 983–990. https://doi.org/10.1080/1369118X.2015.1043320

Bakardjieva, M. (2020). New paradigm or sensitizing concept: Finding the proper place of practice theory in media studies. *International Journal of Communication, 14,* 18.

Becerra, M. (2015). *De la concentración a la convergencia. Políticas de medios en Argentina y América Latina.* Buenos Aires: Paidós.

Becerra, M., & Mastrini, G. (2009). *Los dueños de la palabra. Acceso, estructura y concentración de los medios en la América Latina del Siglo XXI.* Buenos Aires: Prometeo.

Belotti, F. (2020). Are the indigenous media community media? Experiences of native peoples' media practices in Argentina. *Ethnicities, 20*(3), 383–407. https://doi.org/10.1177%2F1468796818810006

Beltrán, L. R. & Reyes, J. (1993). Radio popular en Bolivia: la lucha de obreros y campesinos para democratizar la comunicación. *Diálogos de la Comunicación, 35,* 14–31.

Beltrán, L. R., Herrera, K., Pinto, E. y Torrico, E. (2008). *La comunicación antes de Colón. Tipos y formas en Mesoamérica y los Andes*. La Paz: CIBEC.

Bengoa, J. (2000). *La Emergencia Indígena en América Latina*. Santiago de Chile: Fondo de Cultura Económica.

Bennett, W. L., & Segerberg, A. (2012). The logic of connective action: Digital media and the personalization of contentious politics. *Information, Communication & Society*, *15*(5), 739–768. https://doi.org/10.1080/1369118X.2012.670661

Bernal-Camargo, D. R., & Murillo-Paredes, A. D. (2012). El Acceso de Los Pueblos Indígenas a Las Tecnologías de La Información y La Comunicación En Colombia: ¿Inclusión o Exclusión Social y Política?. *Derecho y Realidad*, *20*, 193–214.

Briones, C. (2003). Mestizaje y blanqueamiento como coordenadas de aboriginalidad y nación en Argentina. *Runa*, *23*(1), 61–88.

Briones, C. (2005). Formaciones de alteridad: contextos globales, procesos nacionales y provinciales. In C. Briones (Eds.). *Cartografías argentinas: Políticas indígenas y formaciones provinciales de alteridad* (pp. 9–39). Buenos Aires: Antropofagia.

Briones, C., & Delrio, W. (2007). La "Conquista del Desierto" desde perspectivas hegemónicas y subalternas. *Runa*, *27*, 23–48.

Busso, N., & Jaimes, D. (2011). *La Cocina de la Ley. El proceso de incidencia en la elaboración de la Ley de Servicios de Comunicación Audiovisual en Argentina*. Buenos Aires: Farco.

CAF– Corporación Andina de Fomento (2020). *Estrategia para la transformación digital de los sectores productivos en América Latina*. Retrieved October 25, 2021 from https://scioteca.caf.com/handle/123456789/1665.

Califano, B. (2019). Urgencias públicas e intereses privados: la regulación de medios en la agenda del gobierno argentino (2015–2019). *Revista Ensambles Primavera*, *6*(11), 72–90.

Carpentier, N. (2007). Four approaches to alternative media. In O. Bailey, B. Cammaerts, & N. Carpentier (Eds.). *Understanding alternative media* (pp. 3–34). Maidenhead: McGraw-Hill Education.

Carpentier, N., & Scifo, S. (2010). Introduction: Community media's long march. *Telematics and Informatics*, *27*(2), 115–118. https://doi.org/10.1016/j.tele.2009.06.006

Carrillo-Olano, A. (2016). Radios comunitarias como forma de resistencia a la homogeneización de la vida. In C. Magallanes-Blanco y J. M. Ramos Rodríguez (Eds.). *Miradas propias. Pueblos indígenas, comunicación y medios en la sociedad global* (pp. 195–213). Puebla, México: Universidad Iberoamericana Puebla.

Carter, D. (2010). Chile's other history: Allende, Pinochet, and redemocratisation in Mapuche perspective. *Studies in Ethnicity and Nationalism*, *10*(1), 59–75. https://doi.org/10.1111/j.1754-9469.2010.01070.x

Cassano, F. (2012). *Southern thought and other essays on the Mediterranean*. New York: Fordham University Press.

Castells, M. (1997). *The power of identity. The information age*. Maiden: Blackwell.

Castells, M. (2009). *Communication power*. Oxford: Oxford University Press.

Castells-Talens, A. (2011). ¿ Ni indígena ni comunitaria? La radio indigenista en tiempos neoindigenistas. *Comunicación y sociedad*, *15*, 123–142.

Castells-Talens, A. (2016). Cuestionando al 'maya permitido': medios, dominación e imaginarios nacionales en la Península de Yucatán. In C. Magallanes-Blanco y J. M. Ramos Rodríguez (Eds.). *Miradas propias. Pueblos indígenas, comunicación y medios en la sociedad global* (pp. 59–89). Puebla: Universidad Iberoamericana Puebla.

Castells-Talens, A., Ramos Rodríguez, J. M. y Chan Concha, M. (2009). Radio, control, and indigenous peoples: The failure of state-invented citizens' media in Mexico. *Development in Practice*, *19*(4), 525–537. https://doi.org/10.1080/09614520902866298

CCAIA– Coordinadora de Comunicación Audiovisual Indígena Argentina (2012). *Comunicación con identidad. Aportes para la construcción del modelo de comunicación indígena en Argentina*. Buenos Aires: CCAIA.

Cerbino, M. (2018). *Por una comunicación del común: medios comunitarios, proximidad y acción*. Quito: Ediciones Ciespal.

Cerbino, M., & Belotti, F. (2018). Between public and private media: Toward a definition of "Community Media." *Latin American Perspectives*, *45*(3), 30–43. https://doi.org/10.1177%2F0094582X18766901

Chawla, D., & Atay, A. (2018). Introduction: Decolonizing autoethnography. *Cultural Studies↔ Critical Methodologies*, *18*(1), 3–8. https://doi.org/10.1177%2F1532708617728955

Collective Author. (2018). *El quehacer de la comunicación desde los pueblos originarios (o cómo no estamos meando fuera de la bacinica)*. Unpublished original text.

Comunello, F., Rosales, A., Mulargia, S., Ieracitano, F., Belotti, F., & Fernández-Ardèvol, M. (2020). 'Youngsplaining' and moralistic judgements: Exploring ageism through the lens of digital 'media ideologies. *Ageing & Society*, 1–24. https://doi.org/10.1017/S0144686X20001312

Connell, R. (2007). The northern theory of globalization. *Sociological Theory*, *25*(4), 368–385. https://doi.org/10.1111%2Fj.1467-9558.2007.00314.x

Córdova, A. (2011). Estéticas enraizadas: Aproximaciones al video indígena en América Latina. *Comunicación y medios*, *24*, 81–107.

Cornejo, I. (2002). *Apuntes para una historia de la radio indigenista en México. Las voces del Mayab*. Ciudad de México: Fundación Buendía.

Cortés, D. M. (2019). Era mejor cuando éramos ilegales (it was better when we were illegals): Indigenous people, the State and public interest indigenous radio stations in Colombia. *Journal of Alternative & Community Media*, *4*(3), 28–42.

Couldry, N., & Curran, J. (Eds.). (2003). *Contesting media power: Alternative media in a networked world*. Rowman & Littlefield Publishers.

Coyer, K., Dowmunt, T., & Fountain, A. (2007). *The alternative media handbook*. London/New York: Routledge.

Croteau, D. (2005). Which side are you on? The tension between movement scholarship and activism. In D. Croteau, W. Hoynes & C. Ryan (Eds.). *Rhyming hope and history: Activists, academics, and social movement scholarship* (pp. 20–40). Minneapolis/London: University of Minnesota Press.

Crotty, M. (1998). *The foundations of social research: Meaning and perspective in the research process*. St Leonards Australia: Allen & Unwin.

Cruz, G. R. (2017). Indigenismo y blanquitud en el orden racista de la Nación. *Intersticios*, *12*, 5–30.

Darder, A. (2018). Decolonizing interpretive research: Subaltern sensibilities and the politics of voice. *Qualitative Research Journal*, *18*(2), 94–104. https://doi.org/10.1108/QRJ-D-17-00056

Datta, R. (2018). Decolonizing both researcher and research and its effectiveness in Indigenous research. *Research Ethics*, *14*(2), 1–24. https://doi.org/10.1177%2F1747016117733296

de la Cadena, M. (2008). *Formaciones de indianidad: Articulaciones raciales, mestizaje y nación en América Latina*. Bogotá: Envión.

de la Cadena, M. (2015). *Earth beings: Ecologies of practice across Andean worlds*. Durham/London: Duke University Press.

de la Peña, G. (1995). La ciudadanía étnica y la reconstrucción de 'los indios' en el México contemporáneo. *Revista Internacional de Filosofía Política*, 6, 116–140.

Della Bruna, D. & Slagter, D. (2019). Escuchar es un acto revolucionario. In D. Andrada (Ed.). *Hacia un periodismo indígena* (pp. 53–66). Buenos Aires: Universidad del Salvador.

Delrio, W. (2010). *Memorias de expropiación. Sometimiento e incorporación indígena en la Patagonia (1872–1943)*. Buenos Aires: UNQ Editorial.

Dennis, J. (2018). *Beyond slacktivism. Political participation on social media*. Cham: Palgrave.

Downing, J. D. (2001). *Radical media: Rebellious communication and social movements*. Thousand Oaks, CA: Sage.

Downing, J. D. (2018). Social movement media and media activism. In J. Nussbaum (Ed.). *Oxford research encyclopedia of communication*. New York/Oxford: Oxford University Press. https://doi.org/10.1093/acrefore/9780190228613.013.574

Doyle, M. (2015a). Debates y demandas indígenas sobre derechos a la comunicación en América Latina. *Temas Antropológicos*, *37*(2), 89–118.

Doyle, M. (2015b, August 27–28). *Los pueblos indígenas en la Ley SCA: antecedentes, transformaciones y desafíos*. Paper presented at the VIII ALAIC regional seminar "Políticas, actores y prácticas de la comunicación: encrucijadas de la investigación en américa latina," Córdoba, Argentina.

Doyle, M. (2016). *El derecho a la comunicación de los pueblos originarios. Límites y posibilidades de las reivindicaciones indígenas en relación al sistema de medios de comunicación en Argentina*. Doctoral Dissertation, Universidad de Buenos Aires, Buenos Aires, Argentina.

Doyle, M. (2018). Las luchas por territorios ancestrales en los medios indígenas. El caso de FM La Voz Indígena. *Comunicación y medios*, *27*(38), 177–189.

Doyle, M. M., & Siares, E. (2018). Indigenous peoples' right to communication with identity in Argentina, 2009–2017. *Latin American Perspectives*, *45*(3), 55–67. https://doi.org/10.1177%2F0094582X18766909

Dutta, M. J., & Pal, M. (2020). Theorizing from the global south: Dismantling, resisting, and transforming communication theory. *Communication Theory*, *30*(4), 349–369. https://doi.org/10.1093/ct/qtaa010

Escobar, A. (2014). *Sentipensar con la tierra. Nuevas lecturas sobre desarrollo, territorio y diferencia*. Medellin: Unaula.

Escobar, A. (2015). Transiciones: A space for research and design for transitions to the pluriverse. *Design Philosophy Papers*, *13*(1), 13–23. https://doi.org/10.1080/14487136.2015.1085690

Espada, A. (2016). Una oportunidad perdida: la ley y los medios sin fines de lucro. In G. Mastrini & M. Becerra (Eds.). *Medios en guerra. Balance, critica y desguace de las políticas de comunicación 2003–2016* (pp. 79–113). Buenos Aires: Biblos.

Farthing, L., & Kohl, B. (2013). Mobilizing memory: Bolivia's enduring social movements. *Social Movement Studies*, *12*(4), 361–376. https://doi.org/10.1080/14742837.2013.807728

Froehling, O. (1997). The cyberspace "war of ink and Internet" in Chiapas, Mexico. *Geographical Review*, *87*(2), 291–307.

Galperin, H. (2017). *Digital society: Gaps and challenges for digital inclusion in Latin America and the Caribbean*. Montevideo: UNESCO.

García-Linera A. (2008). *La potencia plebeya. Acción colectiva e identidades indígenas, obreras y populares en Bolivia*. Buenos Aires: CLACSO-Prometeo.

Garland-Mahler, A. (2017). Global south. In E. O'Brien (Ed.). *Oxford bibliographies in literary and critical theory*. New York: Oxford University Press.

Gerbaudo, P., & Treré, E. (2015). In search of the 'we' of social media activism: Introduction to the special issue on social media and protest identities. *Information, Communication & Society*, *18*(8), 865–871. https://doi.org/10.1080/13691 18X.2015.1043319

Gerlach, A. (2018). Thinking and researching relationally: Enacting decolonizing methodologies with an indigenous early childhood program in Canada. *International Journal of Qualitative Methods*, *17*(1). https://doi.org/10.1177%2F1609406918776075

Ginsburg, F. (1991). Indigenous media: Faustian contract or global village? *Cultural Anthropology*, *6*(1), 92–112.

Ginsburg, F. (1994). Embedded aesthetics: Creating a discursive space for indigenous media. *Cultural Anthropology*, *9*(3), 365–382.

Ginsburg, F. (2011). Native intelligence: A short history of debates on indigenous media and ethnographic film. In M. Banks & J. Ruby (Eds.). *Made to be seen: Perspectives on the history of visual anthropology* (p. 234–55). Chicago/London: University of Chicago Press.

Ginsburg, F. (2016). Indigenous media from U-Matic to YouTube: Media sovereignty in the digital age. *Sociologia & Antropologia*, *6*(3), 581–599. https://doi.org/10.1590/2238-38752016V632

Gómez-Quintero, J. D. (2010). La colonialidad del ser y del saber: la mitologización del desarrollo en América Latina. *El ágora USB*, *10*(1), 87–105.

González-Tanco, E. (2016). *Identidad y empoderamiento para "liberar la palabra." Construcción de un sistema de comunicación indígena en los pueblos originarios del Cauca, Colombia*. Doctoral dissertation, Universidad Complutense de Madrid, Madrid, Spain.

Gordillo, G., & Hirsch, S. (2003). Indigenous struggles and contested identities in Argentina histories of invisibilization and reemergence. *Journal of Latin American Anthropology*, *8*(3), 4–30.

Guest, G., MacQueen, K., & Namey, E. (2011). *Applied thematic analysis*. London: Sage.

Gumucio-Dagron, A. (2001). *Making waves. Participatory communication for social change*. New York: Rockefeller Foundation.

Gumucio-Dagron, A. (2005). Arte de equilibristas: la sostenibilad de los medios de comunicación comunitarios. *Punto Cero, 10*(10), 6–19.

Gutiérrez-Chong, N. (2007). Ethnic origins and indigenous people: An approach from Latin America. In A. Leoussi & S. Grosby (Eds.). *Nationalism and ethnosymbolism: History, culture and ethnicity in the formation of nations* (pp. 312–324). Edinburgh: Edinburgh University Press.

Gutiérrez-Ríos, F. (2014). *We aukiñ zugú. Historia de los medios de comunicación Mapuche*. Santiago de Chile: Quimantú.

Harris, M., Carlson, B., & Poata-Smith, E. (2013). Indigenous identities and the politics of authenticity. In M. Harris, M. Nakata & B. Carlson (Eds.). *The politics of identity: Emerging indigeneity* (pp. 1–9). Sydney: UTS ePress.

Held, M. B. E. (2019). Decolonizing research paradigms in the context of settler colonialism: An unsettling, mutual, and collaborative effort. *International Journal of Qualitative Methods*. https://doi.org/10.1177/1609406918821574

Hernández, I., & Calcagno, S. (2003). Los pueblos indígenas y la sociedad de la información. *Revista argentina de sociología, 1*(1), 110–143.

Hernández, S. A. M. (2020). Digital activism and the Mapuche Nation in Chile. In C. Martens, C. Venegas, & E. F. S. S. Tapuy (Eds.). *Digital activism, community media, and sustainable communication in Latin America* (pp. 221–243). Cham: Palgrave.

Himpele, J. D. (2008). *Circuits of culture: Media, politics and indigenous identity in the Andes*. Minneapolis: University of Minnesota Press.

Howley, K. (2005). *Community media: People, places, and communication technologies*. Cambridge: Cambridge University Press.

Kaplún, M. & García, M. (1987). *El comunicador popular*. Buenos Aires: Lumen.

Kejval, L. (2009). *Truchas: los proyectos político-culturales de las radios comunitarias, alternativas y populares argentinas*. Buenos Aires: Prometeo.

Knoblauch, H. (2019). *The communicative construction of reality*. London: Routledge.

Kovach, M. (2009). *Indigenous methodologies: Characteristics, conversations, and contexts*. Toronto: University of Toronto Press.

Krusz, E., Davey, T., Wigginton, B., & Hall, N. (2020). What contributions, if any, can non-indigenous researchers offer toward decolonizing health research? *Qualitative Health Research, 30*(2), 205–216. https://doi.org/10.1177/1049732319861932

Lenton, D. (2015). Notas para una recuperación de la memoria de las organizaciones de militancia indígena. *Identidades, 8*(5), 117–154.

Lewis, P. J. (2018). What does it mean to be an Ally (Part II). *International Review of Qualitative Research, 11*(1), 46–50. https://doi.org/10.1525%2Firqr.2018.11.1.46

Lizondo, L. (2015). *Comunicación con identidad o comunicación comunitaria. El caso de la FM "La Voz Indígena."* Master's Thesis, Universidad Nacional de La Plata, La Plata, Argentina.

Lizondo, L. (2018). La comunicación con identidad. Regulaciones y un estudio de caso. *Disertaciones, 11*(2), 50–65. https://doi.org/10.12804/revistas.urosario.edu.co/disertaciones/a.5745

Lizondo, L. (2020). *Para una perspectiva del debate naturaleza/cultura desde los medios de comunicación.* Doctoral dissertation, Universidad Nacional de La Plata, La Plata, Argentina.

López, A. J. (2007). Introduction: The (post) Global South. *The Global South, 1*(1), 1–11.

Magallanes-Blanco, C. & Ramos-Rodríguez, J. M. (2016). Introducción. In C. Magallanes-Blanco & J. M. Ramos-Rodríguez (Eds.). *Miradas propias. Pueblos indígenas, comunicación y medios en la sociedad global* (p. 11–15). Puebla: Universidad Iberoamericana Puebla, CIESPAL.

Magallanes-Blanco, C. (2000). Mexico's internal colony. The Zapatista indigenous rebels and their uses of media for de-colonization. *Journal of Imperial and Postcolonial Historical Studies, 1 (1)*, 9–23.

Magallanes-Blanco, C. (2011). Zapatista media [Mexico]. In J. Downing (Ed.). *Encyclopedia of social movement media.* Thousand Oak: Sage.

Magallanes-Blanco, C. (2015). Talking about our mother: Indigenous videos on nature and the environment. *Communication, Culture & Critique, 8*(2), 199–216. https://doi.org/10.1111/cccr.12084

Magallanes-Blanco, C. (forthcoming). Communication from a Latin American indigenous perspective. In F. Subervi (Ed.). *Encyclopedia of race, ethnicity, and communication.* New York/Oxford: Oxford University Press.

Magallanes-Blanco, C., & Monteforte-Bazzarello, G. (2019). Un engagement commun: Des médias autochtones et communautaires pour changer la réalité. In S. Geraud & T. M. Herrmann (Eds.). *Cinémas autochtones: Des représentations en mouvements* (pp. 53–71). Paris: L'Harmattan.

Magallanes-Blanco, C., & Treré, E. (2019). Contemporary social movements and digital media resistance in Latin America 1, 2. In A. C. Pertierra & J. F. Salazar (Eds.). *Media cultures in Latin America* (pp. 110–127). New York: Routledge.

Magallanes-Blanco, C., Solana, T. F., Atala Layún, A. y Parra Hinojosa, D. (2012). Mujeres detrás de la cámara. El proceso de empoderamiento de mujeres indígenas Mixe. In M. I. Patiño Rodríguez-Malpica, M. Ibarra-Mateos & F. J. Sentíes-Laborde (Eds.). *Los rostros de la pobreza. El debate. Tomo VI* (pp. 143–164). Puebla: Universidad Iberoamericana.

Manzanelli, M. (2020). "Somos pueblo, con autodeterminación libre y colectiva" reivindicaciones identitarias-organizativas de Los Chuschagasta y Tolombón. *Tabula Rasa, 34*, 109–130. https://doi.org/10.25058/20112742.n34.06

Marcus, G. (2006). *Connected: Engagements with media.* Chicago: University of Chicago Press.

Margarucci, I. (2019). Moira Millán: "Los medios de comunicación se han encargado de demonizar la imagen de los pueblos originarios." In D. Andrada (Ed.). *Hacia un periodismo indígena* (pp. 163–177). Buenos Aires: Universidad del Salvador.

Marino, S., Mastrini, G., & Becerra, M. (2011). Argentina: el proceso de regulación democrática de la comunicación. In A. Koschützke & E. Gerber (Eds.). *Progresismo y políticas de comunicación. Manos a la obra* (pp. 33–48). Buenos Aires: Fundación Friedrich Ebert.

Martín-Barbero, J. (1981). Prácticas de comunicación en la cultura popular. In M. Simpson (Ed.). *Comunicación alternativa y cambio social* (pp. 32–53). Ciudad de México: UNAM.

Martín-Barbero, J. (2006). *Technicalities, identities, alterities: Changes and opacities of communication in the new century.* Rio de Janeiro: Society Mediated Communication.

Mastrini, G., Becerra, M., & Bizberge, A. (2021). *Grupo Clarín. From Argentine newspaper to convergent media conglomerate.* New York: Routledge.

Mata, M. C. (2006). Comunicación y ciudadanía: problemas teórico-políticos de su articulación. *Revista Fronteiras-estudos midiáticos, 8*(1), 5–15.

Mata, M. C. (2011). Comunicación popular: Continuidades, transformaciones y desafios. *Oficios Terrestres, 26*(26). Retrieved October 25, 2021, from file:/// C:/Users/frabe/Downloads/admin,+Gestor_a+de+la+revista,+156–2113– 1-CE[1].pdf.

Mattoni, A. (2017). A situated understanding of digital technologies in social movements. Media ecology and media practice approaches. *Social Movement Studies, 16*(4), 494–505. https://doi.org/10.1080/14742837.2017.1311250

Mattoni, A. (2020). A media-in-practices approach to investigate the nexus between digital media and activists' daily political engagement. *International Journal of Communication, 14*, 18.

Mattoni, A., & Treré, E. (2014). Media practices, mediation processes, and mediatization in the study of social movements. *Communication Theory, 24*(3), 252–271. https://doi.org/10.1111/comt.12038

May, S. (1998). Language and education rights for indigenous peoples. *Language Culture and Curriculum, 11*(3), 272–296. https://doi.org/10.1080/ 07908319808666557

Mertens, D. M. (2007). Transformative paradigm: Mixed methods and social justice. *Journal of Mixed Methods Research, 1*(3), 212–225. https://doi.org/10.1177 %2F155868980730281

Mignolo, W. (2001). Descolonización epistémica y ética. La contribución de Xavier Albó y Silvia Rivera Cusicanqui a la reestructuración de las ciencias sociales desde los andes. *Rev. Venez. de Econ. y Ciencias Sociales, 7*(3), 175–195.

Mignolo, W. D. (2011). The Global South and world dis/order. *Journal of Anthropological Research, 67*(2), 165–188.

Milan, S. (2016). Liberated technology: inside emancipatory communication activism. In E. Gordon & P. Mihailidis (Eds.). *Civic media: Technology, design, practice* (pp. 107–124). Cambridge/London: MIT Press.

Moreno-Fernández, F. (2006). La diversidad lingüística de Hispanoamérica: implicaciones sociales y políticas. *Boletín Elcano*, (80), 7. Retrieved November 5, 2021 from http://biblioteca.ribei.org/id/eprint/997/.

Murillo, M. A. (2008). Weaving a communication quilt in Colombia: Civil conflict, indigenous resistance, and community radio in Northern Cauca. In P. Wilson & M. Stewart (Eds.). *Global indigenous media. Cultures, poetics, and politics* (pp. 145–159). Raleigh, NC: Duke University Press.

Nakata, M. (2002). Indigenous knowledge and the cultural interface: Underlying issues at the intersection of knowledge and information systems. *IFLA Journal, 28*(5–6), 281–291.

Nakata, M. (2007). The cultural interface. *The Australian Journal of Indigenous Education*, *36*(S1), 7–14. https://doi.org/10.1017/S1326011100004646

Nakata, M. (2013). Identity politics: Who can count as indigenous?. In M. Harris, M., Nakata, & B. Carlson (Eds.). *The politics of identity: Emerging indigeneity* (pp. 125–146). Sydney: UTS epress.

Nicolini, D. (2012). *Practice theory, work, and organization: An introduction.* Oxford: Oxford University Press.

Otero, J. V. (2008). *El Derecho a la Comunicación en el Plan de Vida de los Pueblos Indígenas del Cauca.* Bogotá: Centro de Competencia en Comunicación para América Latina – FES.

Quijano, A. (2000). Coloniality of power and Eurocentrism in Latin America. *International Sociology*, *15*(2), 215–232. https://doi.org/10.1177%2F0268580900015002005

Ramos-Martín, J. (2018). Los medios comunitarios indígenas como construcción de memoria en resistencia en Bolivia. *América Latina Hoy*, 78, 17–36. https://doi.org/10.14201/alh2018781736

Ramos-Rodríguez, J. M. (2016). Radio, cultura e identidad: 10 tesis sobre la radio indigenista mexicana. In C. Magallanes-Blanco y J. M. Ramos Rodríguez (Eds.). *Miradas propias. Pueblos indígenas, comunicación y medios en la sociedad global* (pp. 179–193). Puebla: Universidad Iberoamericana Puebla.

Ramos-Rodríguez, J. M. (2020). *Are indigenous voices being heard? A study on the state of indigenous community broadcasting in 19 countries.* Cambridge/Toronto: Cultural Survival/WACC.

RICCAP– Red de Investigación en Comunicación Comunitaria, Alternativa y Participativa (2019). *Relevamiento de los servicios de comunicación audiovisual comunitarios, populares, alternativos, cooperativos y de pueblos originarios en argentina.* Buenos Aires: Riccap.

Rivera-Cusicanqui, S. (1986). *Oprimidos pero no vencidos: luchas del campesinado aymara y qhechwa de Bolivia, 1900–1980.* Geneva: Instituto de Investigaciones de las Naciones Unidas para el Desarrollo Social.

Rivera-Cusicanqui, S. (2008). El potencial epistemológico y teórico de la historia oral: de la lógica instrumental a la descolonización de la historia. In A. Rosillo-Martínez et al. (Eds.). *Teoria crítica dos direitos humanos no século XXI* (pp. 154–175). Porto Alegre: EDIPUCRS.

Rivera-Cusicanqui, S. (2018). *Un mundo ch'ixi es posible. Ensayos desde un presente en crisis.* Buenos Aires: Tinta Limón.

Rodríguez, C. (2001). *Fissures in the mediascape: An international study of citizens' media.* Cresskill, N.J: Hampton Press.

Rodríguez, C., & El Gazi, J. (2007). The poetics of indigenous radio in Colombia. *Media, Culture & Society*, *29*(3), 449–468. https://doi.org/10.1177%2F0163443707076185

Rodríguez, C., Ferron, B., & Shamas, K. (2014). Four challenges in the field of alternative, radical and citizens' media research. *Media, Culture & Society*, *36*(2), 150–166. https://doi.org/10.1177%2F0163443714523877

Russell, A. (2005). Myth and the Zapatista movement: Exploring a network identity. *New Media & Society*, *7*(4), 559–577. https://doi.org/10.1177%2F1461444805054119

Ryan, C. (2005). Successful collaboration: Movement building in the media arena. In D. Croteau, W. Hoynes & C. Ryan (Eds.). *Rhyming hope and history: Activists, academics, and social movement scholarship* (pp. 115–136). Minneapolis/ London: University of Minnesota Press.

Salazar, J. (2002). Activismo indígena en américa latina: Estrategias para una construcción cultural de las tecnologías de información y comunicación. *Journal of Iberian and Latin American Studies*, *8* (2), 61–79. https://doi.org/10.1080/13260 219.2002.10431783

Salazar, J. F. & Córdova, A. (2008). Imperfect media and the poetics of indigenous video in Latin America. In P. Wilson y M. Stewart (Eds.). *Global indigenous media. Culture, poetics and politics* (pp. 39–57). Raleigh, NC: Duke University Press.

Salazar, J. F. (2003). Articulating an activist imaginary: Internet as counter public sphere in the Mapuche movement, 1997/2002. *Media International Australia*, *107*(1), 19–30.

Salazar, J. F. (2010). Making culture visible: The mediated construction of a Mapuche nation in Chile. In C. Rodríguez, D. Kidd & L. Stein (Eds.). *Making our media: Global initiatives toward a democratic public sphere. Vol. 1: Creating new communication spaces* (pp. 29–46). Cresskill: Hampton Press.

Salazar, J. F. (2014). Prácticas de auto-representación y los dilemas de la auto-determinación: el cara y sello de los derechos a la comunicación Mapuche." In C. Barrientos (Ed.). *Aproximaciones a la cuestión mapuche en Chile, una mirada desde la historia y las ciencias sociales* (pp. 143–160). Santiago: RIL.

Salazar, J. F. (2015). Social movements and video indígena in Latin America: Key challenges for 'anthropologies otherwise'. In S. Pink & S. Abram (Eds.). *Media, anthropology and public engagement* (pp. 122–143). New York: Berghahn Books.

Salazar, J. F., & Córdova, A. (2019). Indigenous media cultures in Abya Yala. In A. C. Pertierra, & J. F. Salazar (Eds.). *Media cultures in Latin America: Key concepts and new debates* (pp. 128–146). New York: Routledge.

Salazar, J.F. (2009). Self-determination in practice: The critical making of indigenous media. *Development in Practice* 19(4), 504–513. https://doi. org/10.1080/09614520902866397

Sandoval-Forero, E. A. (2013). Los indígenas en el ciberespacio. *Agricultura, sociedad y desarrollo*, *10*(2), 235–256.

Santos, B. d-S. (2018). *The end of the cognitive empire: The coming of age of epistemologies of the south*. Durham/London: Duke University Press.

Santos, B. d-S., & Meneses, M. P. (Eds.). (2019). *Knowledges born in the struggle: Constructing the epistemologies of the global south*. New York: Routledge.

Schatzki, T. R. (1997). Practices and actions: A Witgensteinian critique of Bourdieu and Giddens. *Philosophy of the Social Sciences*, *27*(3), 283–308. https://doi.org/1 0.1177%2F004839319702700301

Schiwy, F. (2002). La otra mirada. Video indígena y descolonización. In C. Walsh, F. Schiwy & S. Castro-Gómez (Eds.). *Indisciplinar las Ciencias Sociales Geopolíticas del conocimiento y colonialidad del poder. Perspectivas desde lo Andino* (pp. 101–134), Quito: Universidad Andina Simón Bolívar, Abya-Yala.

Schiwy, F. (2003). Descolonizar las tecnologías del conocimiento: video y epistemología indígena. En C. Walsh (Ed.). *Estudios culturales latinoamericanos*.

Retos desde y sobre la región andina (pp. 303–313). Quito: Universidad Andina Simón Bolívar, Abya-Yala.

Schiwy, F. (2009). *Indianizing film. Decolonization, the Andes, and the question of technology*. Newark: Rutgers University Press.

Schiwy, F. (2016). ¿Hay un común posible? En C. Magallanes-Blanco y J. M. Ramos Rodríguez (Eds.). *Miradas propias. Pueblos indígenas, comunicación y medios en la sociedad global* (pp. 17–43). Puebla: Universidad Iberoamericana Puebla.

Schiwy, F. (2018). Decolonization and collaborative media: A Latin American perspective. In J. Nussbaum (Ed.). *Oxford research encyclopedia of communication*. New York/Oxford: Oxford University Press. https://doi.org/10.1093/acrefore/9780190228613.013.641

Schiwy, F., & Weber, B. W. (Eds.). (2017). *Adjusting the lens: Community and collaborative video in Mexico*. Pittsburgh: University of Pittsburgh Press.

Scifo, S. (2015). Technology, empowerment and community radio. *Mídia e Cotidiano, 7*(7): 84–111. Retrieved October 25, 2021 from http://eprints.bournemouth.ac.uk/23573/.

Segura, M. S., & Waisbord, S. (2016). *Media movements: Civil society and media policy reform in Latin America*. London: Zed Books Ltd.

Servindi – Servicios en Comunicación Intercultural (2008). *Comunicación y comunicadores indígenas*. Lima: Servindi.

Shove, E., Pantzar, M., & Watson M. (2012). *The dynamics of social practice: Everyday life and how it changes*. London: SAGE.

Sierra-Caballero, F., & Gravante, T. (Eds.). (2017). *Networks, movements and technopolitics in Latin America: Critical analysis and current challenges*. Cham: Palgrave.

Smith, L. C. (2006). Mobilizing indigenous video: The Mexican case. *Journal of Latin American Geography, 5*(1), 113–128.

Smith, L. C. (2016). Algunas geografías de videos indígenas hechos en Oaxaca, México. In C. Magallanes-Blanco y J. M. Ramos Rodríguez (Eds.). *Miradas propias. Pueblos indígenas, comunicación y medios en la sociedad global* (pp. 111–131). Puebla: Universidad Iberoamericana Puebla.

Soler, C. (2017). "Enfocar nuestra trinchera." El surgimiento del cine indígena en la provincia del Chaco (Argentina). *Folia Histórica del Nordeste, 28*, 71–97.

Soler, C. (2019). *Cine comunitario y soberanía visual entre los qom (tobas) del chaco argentino*. Doctoral Dissertation, Universidad de Buenos Aires and École des hautes études en sciences sociales, Buenos Aires (Argentina) and Paris (France).

Spitulnik, D. (1993). Anthropology and mass media. *Annual Review of Anthropology, 22*(1), 293–315. https://doi.org/10.1146/annurev.an.22.100193.001453

Stavenhagen, R. (1997). Las organizaciones indígenas: actores emergentes en América Latina. *Revista de la CEPAL, 62*, 61–73.

Stephansen, H. C. (2017). Media activism as movement? Collective identity formation in the orld Forum of Free Media. *Media and Communication, 5*(3), 59–66. https://doi.org/10.17645/mac.v5i3.1034

Stephenson, M. (2002). Forging an indigenous counterpublic sphere: The Taller de Historia Oral Andina in Bolivia. *Latin American Research Review*, 99–118.

Svampa, M. (2016). *Debates latinoamericanos. Indianismo, desarrollo, dependencia, populismo.* Cochabamba: Centro de Documentación e Información, Edhasa.

Tarica, E. (2016). Indigenismo. In W. H. Beezley (Ed.). *Oxford research encyclopedia of Latin American history.* New York/Oxford: Oxford University Press. https://doi.org/10.1093/acrefore/9780199366439.013.68

Teuber, B. (1996). De la colonización alfabética considerada como una de las artes del sujeto. *Nueva Revista de Filología Hispánica, 44*(2), 541–554.

Thompson, L., & Tapscott, C. (Eds.). (2010). *Citizenship and social movements: Perspectives from the global south.* London/New York: Zed Books.

Todd, B. (2013). Reparar el silencio: justicia para los daños lingüísticos causados por colonización y conflicto. *Revista de Derecho Público, 31*, 1–39.

Treré, E. (2019). *Hybrid media activism: Ecologies, imaginaries, algorithms.* London/New York: Routledge.

Trerè, E., & Magallanes-Blanco, C. (2015). Battlefields, experiences, debates: Latin American struggles and digital media resistance: Introduction. *International Journal of Communication, 9*, 3652–3661.

Trere, E., & Pleyers, G. (2015). A conversation with Geoffrey Pleyers: The battlefields of Latin American struggles and the challenges of the internet for social change. *International Journal of Communication, 9*, 3814–3822.

Trinchero, H. H. (2009). Pueblos originarios y políticas de reconocimiento en Argentina. *Papeles de Trabajo, 18*: 1–17.

Tuhiwai-Smith, L. (1999). *Decolonizing methodologies: Research and indigenous peoples.* London: Zed Books.

Tuhiwai-Smith, L. (2006). Choosing the margins. In K. Denzin & D. Giardina (Eds.). *Qualitative inquiry and the conservative challenge* (pp. 151–173). Walnut Creek: Left Coast Press.

Turner, T. (1992). Defiant images: The Kayapo appropriation of video. *Anthropology Today, 8*(6), 5–16. https://doi.org/10.2307/2783265

Turner, T. (1995). Representation, collaboration and mediation in contemporary ethnographic and indigenous media. *Visual Anthropology Review, 11*(2), 102–106. https://doi.org/10.1525/var.1995.11.2.102

Veronelli, G. A. (2015). The coloniality of language: Race, expressivity, power, and the darker side of modernity. *Wagadu: A Journal of Transnational Women's & Gender Studies, 13*. Retrieved November 5, 2021 from http://sites.cortland.edu/wagadu/wp-content/uploads/sites/3/2015/07/5-FIVE-Veronelli.pdf.

Viatori, M., & Ushigua, G. (2007). Speaking sovereignty: Indigenous languages and self-determination. *Wicazo Sa Review, 22*(2), 7–21.

Vinelli, N. (2010). Alternative media heritage in Latin America. In J. D. Downing. (Ed.), *Encyclopedia of social movement media* (pp. 27–30). Thousand Oaks, CA: Sage.

Vinelli, N. (2014). *La televisión desde abajo. Historia, alternatividad y periodismo de contrainformación.* Buenos Aires: Editorial Cooperativa El Río Suena, El Topo Blindado.

Wahnish, G. (2019). Relmu Ñamku: "La comunicación es una de las armas y herramientas más fuertes para presionar a los gobiernos para reformar sus políticas." In D. Andrada (Ed.). *Hacia un periodismo indígena* (pp. 149–162). Buenos Aires: Universidad del Salvador.

Walsh, C.E. (2018). Decoloniality in/as praxis. Part 1. In W. D. Mignolo & C. E. Walsh (Eds). *On decoloniality. Concepts, analytics, praxis.* Durham/London: Duke University Press.

Weise, C., & Álvarez, I. M. (2018). Identidad y percepciones de género. Retos para la formación de mujeres líderes indígenas. *Aposta. Revista de Ciencias Sociales*, *77*, 257–287.

Wellman, B. (2004). The three ages of internet studies: Ten, five and zero years ago. *New Media & Society*, *6*(1), 123–129. https://doi.org/10.1177 %2F1461444804040633

Whyte, K. P. (2011). The recognition dimensions of environmental justice in Indian country. *Environmental Justice*, *4*(4), 199–205. https://doi.org/10.1089/ env.2011.0036

Whyte, K. P. (2016). Indigenous experience, environmental justice and settler colonialism. In B. E. Bannon (Ed.). *Nature and experience: Phenomenology and the environment* (pp. 157–174). New York: Rowman & Littlefield

Williams, R., & Edge, D. (1996). The social shaping of technology. *Research Policy*, *25*(6), 865–899. https://doi.org/10.1016/0048-7333(96)00885-2

Wilson, P. (2015). Indigenous media: Linking the local, translocal, global and virtual. In S. P. Mains, J. Cupples, & C. Lukinbeal (Eds.). *Mediated geographies and geographies of media* (pp. 367–383). Dordrecht: Springer.

Wilson, P., & Stewart, M. (2008). Introduction: Indigeneity and indigenous media on the global stage. In P. Wilson & M. Stewart (Eds.). *Global indigenous media. Cultures, poetics, and politics* (pp. 1–36). Raleigh: Duke University Press.

Wilson, P., Hearne, J., Córdova, A., & Thorner, S. (2014). Indigenous media. *Oxford Bibliographies*, 1–1. https://doi.org/10.1093/OBO/9780199791286-0229

Wilson, S. (2001). What is Indigenous research methodology? *Canadian Journal of Native Education*, *25*(1), 175–179.

Worth, S., & Adair, J. (1972). *Through Navajo eyes: An exploration of film communication and anthropology*. Bloomington: Indiana University Press.

Wortham, E. (2004). Between state and indigenous autonomy: Unpacking video indígena in Mexico. *American Anthropologist*, *2*(106): 363–367. https://doi. org/10.1525/aa.2004.106.2.363

Wortham, E. (2013). *Indigenous media in Mexico. Culture, vommunity, and the state*. Durham/London Duke University Press.

Yanniello, F. (2014). *Descolonizando la palabra. Los medios de comunicación del pueblo Mapuche en Puelmapu*. La Plata: La Caracola.

Zamorano-Villarreal, G. (2009). *Reimagining politics: Video and indigenous struggles in contemporary Bolivia*. Doctoral dissertation, University of New York, New York.

Zamorano-Villarreal, G. (2014). Crafting contemporary indigeneity through audiovisual media in Bolivia." In H. Gilbert & C. Gleghorn (Eds.). *Recasting commodity and spectacle in the indigenous Americas* (pp. 77–96). London: ILAS.

Zamorano-Villarreal, G. (2017). *Indigenous media and political imaginaries in contemporary Bolivia*. Lincoln: University of Nebraska Press.

Index

For Product Safety Concerns and Information please contact our EU
representative GPSR@taylorandfrancis.com
Taylor & Francis Verlag GmbH, Kaufingerstraße 24, 80331 München, Germany

www.ingramcontent.com/pod-product-compliance
Lightning Source LLC
Chambersburg PA
CBHW061753270326
41928CB00011B/2485